THE BOOKE OF
GOSTLYE GRACE
OF
MECHTILD OF HACKEBORN

Edited by

THERESA A. HALLIGAN

PONTIFICAL INSTITUTE OF MEDIAEVAL STUDIES

TORONTO

STUDIES AND TEXTS

46

THE BOOKE OF
GOSTLYE GRACE
OF
MECHTILD OF HACKEBORN

EDITED BY

THERESA A. HALLIGAN

PONTIFICAL INSTITUTE OF MEDIAEVAL STUDIES
TORONTO, 1979

ACKNOWLEDGMENT

This book has been published with
a grant in aid of publication from
the De Rancé Foundation.

CANADIAN CATALOGUING IN PUBLICATION DATA

Mechthild, of Hackeborn, 1241 or 2-1299?
  The Booke of gostlye grace of Mechtild of Hackeborn

(Studies and texts — Pontifical Institute of Mediaeval Studies ; 46 ISSN 0082-5328)

Middle English translation of Liber spiritualis gratiae.
The Liber spiritualis gratiae is more correctly known as the Liber specialis gratiae ;
it consists of revelations and devotions transmitted in writing by two sisters, one of
whom was, in all probability, Gertrude the Great.

Bibliography: p.
Includes index.
ISBN 0-88844-046-4

1. Spiritual life — Middle Ages, 600-1500.
I. Gertrude, Saint, surnamed the Great, 1256-1302?
II. Halligan, Theresa A., 1926-   III. Title. IV. Series: Pontifical Institute of
Mediaeval Studies. Studies and texts — Pontifical Institute of Mediaeval Studies;
46.

BX2349.M3313   248   C78-001621-1

© 1979
PONTIFICAL INSTITUTE OF MEDIAEVAL STUDIES
59 Queen's Park Crescent East
Toronto, Ontario, Canada M5S 2C4

PRINTED BY UNIVERSA, WETTEREN, BELGIUM

Contents

Acknowledgments

It is a pleasure to record here my deep appreciation to those who have aided me in the preparation of this edition. I acknowledge with gratitude my debt to Dr. Gabriel M. Liegey, Professor Emeritus of Fordham University, for directing my initial version of this work and later for offering valuable suggestions concerning the arrangement of the text. I am indebted also to Rev. Edmund Colledge, O.S.A., and Dr. A. I. Doyle for their unstinting kindness and generosity in responding to my frequent requests for advice and information. In matters involving German and Latin readings I have been greatly helped by Rev. John J. Halligan, S.J., Dr. Ilse Reis, the late Rev. Herbert Musurillo, S.J., and Rev. Peter J. Torpy, S.J.

I am obliged to the authorities of the British libraries cited in this edition who have permitted me to make use of the manuscripts in their holdings. For friendly service over the years I thank the staff of Fordham University Library, particularly Miss Anne Murphy, Director, and Miss Anne Finnan.

Special mention is due to Miss Virginia E. Smith for her skillful assistance in preparing the final typescript and for her consistent cheerfulness in the face of an often cheerless task. Finally, I express my profound gratitude to my husband, Dr. George B. Pepper, for his long-term sympathy and encouragement.

Abbreviations

EETS OS	Early English Text Society. Original Series
EETS ES	Early English Text Society. Extra Series.
JEGP	Journal of English and Germanic Philology.
MED	Middle English Dictionary.
OED	Oxford English Dictionary.
P.L.	Patrologiae Latinae Cursus Completus.

1

The Manuscripts

A. *THE BOOKE OF GOSTLYE GRACE*

This is the Middle English translation of *Liber Spiritualis Gratiae*,[1] the revelations of Mechtild of Hackeborn, a thirteenth-century mystic of the Benedictine convent in Helfta, Germany. The work survives in two fifteenth-century manuscripts.

OXFORD, BODLEIAN LIBRARY, MS BODLEY (220 (B)

Partly parchment, partly paper;[2] about $11^1/_2 \times 8^1/_2$ in.; 112 uneven leaves + two flyleaves pasted to the covers. Fifteenth-century writing by one scribe throughout is small but rarely illegible. Single columns of text enclosed by light vertical and horizontal rulings, 36-41 lines to a page; seven quires of sixteen leaves, usually but not always to two inner and two outer folios are parchment; catchwords, no signatures. Binding, probably not original, of plain white sheepskin over boards, both damaged by rust. Several words on the first three folios partly obliterated by rust holes.

Latin passages are in red, as are the large unflourished capital letters, some ornamented in green, at the beginnings of chapters. Red is used also for headings, titles, chapter numbers, underlining, and sporadically for punctuation, rubrics, paragraph marks, and for decorating small capitals within a chapter. These red touches are frequent on any given page. On the top of the inside front cover is "Ihesu. Sit deus in primis adiutor hijs et in imis. Maria et Iohannes"; lower down "wyche" is written twice. Inside the back cover is "In dei nomine."

---

[1] The correct title is *Liber Specialis Gratiae*. "Spiritualis" is a misinterpretation of the abbreviated "Specialis." Throughout this edition *Liber* will be used to refer to the Latin account, *Booke* to the Middle English version, and revelations to the work in general.

[2] Three different watermarks on ff. 14, 59, 109 are similar but not identical to designs dated from about the middle to the third quarter of the century in C. M. Briquet, *Les Filigranes* (Paris, 1907), nos. 14900, 14394, 15068.

Contents are all in English: *The Boke of Gostely Grace* (ff. 1^r-101^r); a treatise on meekness[3] (ff. 101^r-103^r) beginning "Seynt Gregour the doctour seith that withouten mekenes it is vnlefulle to trust of forgeuenesse of thy synne," and concluding "Deo gracias Amen. quod Wellys I. et cetera";[4] "The gadred counseiles off the wordes off seynt Isidre to enforme man how he shuld flee vices and ffolow vertues"[5] (ff. 103^r-106^r); and two English poems beginning "Why ys þe world belouyd þat fals ys and veyn" (f. 106^r-106^v); and "Erthe oute of erthe ys wonderly wrought" (ff. 106^v-107^r).[6] Ff. 107^v-112^v are blank.

The *Boke* is complete, comprising a Table of Chapters, the translator's prologue, two general prologues, five parts with numbered chapters, and the translator's epilogue. Headings in Latin identify the parts through f. 16, again on ff. 40^v-41^r and ff. 56^v-57^r. The margins of the first 20 leaves are cluttered with corrections, arabic digits corresponding to the roman numbering of chapters in the text, and rubrics—all in the same hand as the text. These notes start to dwindle on f. 20^r and all but disappear after f. 51^r. Many errors in the text have been corrected by the scribe in the course of his writing, the most conspicuous of which are the profusion of solitary cancelled letters, or half-formed letters, indicating that the writer noticed that he had skipped a word after forming the initial letter of the word ahead. Some of these cancellations are difficult to distinguish from the many other stray slashes denoting pauses

---

[3] The treatise is partly based on St. Bernard. A. I. Doyle, "A Text Attributed to Ruusbroec Circulating in England," in *Dr. L. Reypens-Album*, ed. Alb. Ampe, s.j. (Antwerp, 1964), p. 160, notes that ten known copies are adapted variously for a brother or sister. This version is addressed to "brothere or sistere (sustere)" three times on f. 101^v. The ten copies are listed in P. S. Jolliffe, *A Check-List of Middle English Prose Writings of Spiritual Guidance* (Toronto, 1974), item G. 19.

[4] The name is too common for certain identification. However, in view of the evidence discussed in Chapter 3 of this Introduction showing Carthusian sponsorship of Mechtild's revelations, it is worth noting that in 1425 one John Wells, a monk of the House of the Salutation in London started a series of moves to other Charterhouses in England: in 1427 he was at Hull; in 1439 he was about to leave Mount Grace for another Charterhouse in the province. The obit for a John Wellis, monk of Hinton Charterhouse, who might be the same person, is recorded in 1445. See E. Margaret Thompson, *The Carthusian Order in England* (London, 1930), p. 284.

[5] A version of this piece from ms Harley 1706 was edited by C. Horstman, *Yorkshire Writers: Richard Rolle of Hampole and His Followers*, 2 vols. (London, 1895-6), 2: 367-74. Jolliffe, *Check-List*, item I. 22 (c) lists 14 copies.

[6] Other texts of these poems appear in *Hymns to the Virgin and Christ, The Parliament of Devils, and other Religious Poems*, ed. F. J. Furnivall (EETS 24, 1895), pp. 86, 88. Hilda M. R. Murray's edition of *Erthe upon Erthe* (EETS 141, 1911) does not include B's copy among the 24 variants printed. Rosemary Woolf refers to both poems at several points in *The English Religious Lyric in the Middle Ages* (Oxford, 1968). See C. Brown and R. H. Robbins, *The Index of Middle English Verse* (New York, 1943), nos. 3939, 4160.

or marks resulting from the scribe resting his pen. The abrupt cessation of corrections in the margins and the numerous undetected omissions and repetitions in the second half of the manuscript point to an unfinished re-reading.

The script, though often cramped, is generally clear. Capitalization is used more freely than is the modern practice. Double *f* is written for the capital letter; there is no distinction between *I* and *J*. The letters þ and *y* are clearly differentiated, the latter often dotted in final position, sometimes elsewhere too. Words with prefix *a-* are usually disjuncted: "a byde," "a ȝens," "a redye," "a mong."

Red paragraph marks separate the run-on entries in the Table of Chapters; they are used within the chapters of the *Boke* to divide contents, often to introduce direct quotation and to enclose at the end of a new line the leftover passage concluding the preceding chapter. Punctuation marks in black or red are confined to points and light oblique strokes, the former very common for full stops although there is no consistent practice. The double slanted dash is often but not invariably used as a hyphen at ends of lines after a word is broken. After Latin passages there is often a double or even a triple dash.

The contractions "þᵗ," "þᵘ," "wᵗ" appear and so do their expanded forms "þat," "þou," "with."

Final *h* and double *l* are generally crossed, apparently as a habit and without significance. A fine slanted hair stroke is used over almost all *i-n* and *n-i* combinations; sometimes a light curved stroke occurs over *i* elsewhere: "îs," "obedîence," "þîs," "worshîp," "ȝît."

The usual signs of abbreviation are used for *-er, -us, -ur*, and for *par-, pre-, pri-, pro-*. The loop is a sign for *-es*, the common inflexional syllable in this manuscript. A line attached to and curving up and over final *-r, -g*, sometimes *-n*, indicates a following *-e*. The similar mark attached to a final vowel as well as the separate straight or curved horizontal stroke over the vowel in any position is used for a following nasal. In words ordinarily ending in *-ion* this mark often stands for the missing *-i*: "affliccôn," "deuocôn," but it is written thoughtlessly too: "passyôns" (*-ioun* is absent). A superscript *u* over the nasal in *u-n* combinations indicates an intervening *a* as in "euñgeliste." The usual sign for *-ur-* sometimes takes on the office of general contraction: "nˊligentes" ("necligentes"), "confessouˊs" ("confessoures").

LONDON, BRITISH LIBRARY, MS EGERTON 2006 (E)

Vellum; $10 \times 6^3/_4$ in.; 212 leaves + two flyleaves pasted to the covers. Written throughout in one fifteenth-century book hand. Light vertical and horizontal rulings outline the single columns of text; early folios average 36 lines to a page, but this number gradually reduces to 32 lines; the first 26 gatherings, marked in combinations of symbols or letters with roman numerals, are in eights; the 27th has four leaves. Medieval leather binding over boards, clasp missing, remnants of nail heads; worm holes have penetrated the borads, flyleaves, and the last three folios.

Initial letters of each entry in the Table of Chapters are alternately red and blue; in the text blue is reserved for the flourished letter at the beginning of each chapter, red for the rubrics. Some capitals have not been filled in, but small guide letters are visible. The initial capital on f. 1^r and those at the outset of each of the five parts are very elaborate, ranging from two to seven lines in depth and with trailing ornaments along half the page.

On the first flyleaf are written in a contemporary hand (but not the scribe's) "Anne warrewyk" and "R Gloucestre" [Richard III],[7] and in another hand of later date "lying legend als [?] Romante [?] de Sancte Matilde." On the last flyleaf are "R gloucestre" again, the seventeenth-century signatures of Bessy Harrimons of Wenlock and Edward Holland[8] of Sidnall, Latin ejaculations, some scrawled letters, and some doodlings.

Partially legible signatures and scribblings appear in lower margins on f. 85^r: "Elizaabeth Maior, Eneanor ffruene, Eliz M" (sixteenth or seventeenth century); f. 127^r: "Marget Thorpe [?]" (fifteenth century); f. 206^r: "If the tax & the pole last but on yoear ar to more wee neuer need feear the french land on ouer shore for fear of the carg of mantaine—[?] the carg of the poore" (seventeenth century); f. 211^v upper margin: "To hys lovynge ffrende [?] Thomas Gatacre" (late sixteenth century); f. 212^r after the explicit in two different hands: "Fynis huius libri" and "To his lovinge T. G. [?]." Other marginalia in several different hands consist of about two dozen rubrics in Latin and English, a few arabic digits corresponding to or correcting roman numbers of chapters, an occasional *Nota* or *Nota Bene*, and several crude drawings of a trifoliate leaf.

The volume contains only *The Booke of Gostlye Grace* (f. 1^r-212^r) which follows B exactly except that lengthy rubrics—nearly verbatim duplications of items in the Table of Chapters—are prefixed to the chapters within the text.

The handwriting is large, round, and consistently legible. Cancellations

---

[7] The signature is not Richard's, but it is possible that the book belonged to his wife, Anne Warwick, whom he married in 1471. The couple spent much time in their Yorkshire home, Middleham Castle in Wensleydale. Both persons died in 1485. Richard and Edward IV were the sons of Cicely of York (1415-95), a woman of extraordinary piety. Her library of spiritual readings included the revelations of "St. Maude" [Mechtild]. See C. A. J. Armstrong, "The Piety of Cicely, Duchess of York," in *For Hilaire Belloc*, ed. Douglas Woodruff (New York, 1942), pp. 75-82; andd below, p.. 51, items 18 and 19.

[8] Owner of the manuscript in the seventeenth century.

and erasures are very rare; one has the impression that the scribe was reluctant to spoil the appearance of a neat page. The ink is clear; only notations in the margins are faded and they are obviously in ink of a different composition.

There is no confusion between þ and y; sometimes the y is dotted. I and J are not distinguished and ff is used for F. Capital letters follow full stops, but they appear elsewhere unsystematically, notably in several words on the top line of a leaf, and once even in mid-word "vnchauniable" 431/9. Conjunction and disjunction reflect scribal caprice: "begoddys in spyracion," "lord ys faace," "goddissone."

Each entry in the Table of Chapters and each chapter in the *Booke* proper begins on a new line, but rubrics run on directly after the conclusion of the preceding chapters. There are no signs of paragraph divisions within the chapters.

The point and the light oblique stroke are used for punctuation. Together or separately they are full stops after each entry in the Table of Chapters and after the rubrics, although sometimes the double point is employed. In the *Booke* a single point is usually used for the same purpose, but it is sometimes omitted and is used erratically in other places, e.g., before and after numerals, Latin fragments, and the name of Jesus. More consistently, the slanted double dash is used at the ends of lines to hyphenate broken words.

Besides the usual contractions "þᵗ," "wᵗ," "þᵘ" (here interpreted to be "þou" since that is more frequent than "þowe") the scribe occasionally employs "hˢ," "hᵗ," "þˢ" for "his," "hit," and "þis." "Þᵉ" also appears as does final s superscript squeezed in at the end of a line.

A stroke through the final double l and through h in final -ch indicates a following e which is always present when the letters are not stroked. But the stroked h in -ght or -th ("nyght," "begynneth," "comforthe") and the stroked l in -bl or -pl combinations ("noble," "discyple" and in the suffix -able) are without significance.

The light oblique stroke usually is seen over i in roman numerals, over i-n or n-i groups, sometimes over i-m, but not over other minim letters, e.g., "vnnumerable" 262/6.

Like B, the usual symbols convey -us and syllables with r. The loop in final position is taken to mean -es since that inflexion is written more often than -is, -ys. The curl hooking back over final r indicates a following -e.

The horizontal line, either straight or slightly curved, over a vowel (and sometimes extending over neighboring letters) represents a missing nasal. The same stroke over a nasal signals a following -e. However, there is evidence that the stroke is purely mechanical, e.g., "nomen̄" 492/5, "hym̄" 245/3 (never "hyme").

In words ending elsewhere in -ion, -ioun, the horizontal stroke might indicate the omission of *i*, or perhaps *n* or *u* because it is difficult to tell whether the scribe wrote -*oū* or -*oñ*: "delectacoñs," "conuersacoñ," "vnyoū," "perfeccioñ." An *e* after this syllable is very rare.

Another uncertainty is the function of a superscript letter resembling *u*. Usually this symbolizes *ra*-, but over *u-n* it indicates a missing *a* or *au* "euñgeliste," "obserũnce." It is also employed where no suspension is possible and is clearly redundant: "auñtere," "brauñches," "chauñched," "pennauñce," repentauñce." It might merely call attention to -*un*-combinations but its use in this function is by no means consistent.

Relationship of the Middle English Manuscripts

The only sustained difference between B and E is the presence of rubrics preceding chapters in E. Otherwise the manuscripts are uniform. It is certain that both are copies since they abound in the usual errors associated with the mechanics of transcribing: (1) misinterpretation or alteration of the exemplar, (2) omission by homoeoteleuton, i.e., eye-slip, (3) repetition either by recurrence of adjacent material or by intrusion of passages from nearby contexts.[9] But they are not closely related for each has misreadings and omissions not duplicated in the other.

It is unlikely that errors common to both manuscripts are independent and coincidental mistakes. The probability is strong that B and E are independently descended from an earlier copy already slightly corrupted. Both have mutual misreadings: "worscheppede" for "washed" 26/1, 62/16, "of" for "if" 46/2, 473/15, "lyght" for "height" 107/15, "sowne" for "seem" 134/19, "be" for "berye" (bury) 166/21, "þat" for "þan" 376/20, "syght" for "plyght" 449/7, and possibly "herte" for "heede" 607/4; omissions: "herte" 31/22, 32/11, "noble" 134/9, "of God" 169/5, "haffe in mynde" 309/14, "commemoracion" 325/12; misplacements: "in here breste" 24/3; "þat es to saye þe luffe & desyre" 201/15, "of his lorde" 213/11, "ande childehede" 277/1, "goode" 281/17, and the long passage stated in the

---

[9] Some examples of these mistakes in B: (1) "bad" for "ladde" 23/6, "wynd" for "vyne" 34/18, "ordre" for "othere" 80/18, "partyes" for "propertes" 89/5, "lyȝt" for "hye" 90/8, "nouȝt vndyrstondynge" for "noughtwithstondynge" 154/12, "fawtes" for "sawtez" 159/8, "helpe" for "heepe" 293/7, "clere" for "chere" 457/2, "wagerynge" for "waver—" 529/21; (2) 12/9-10, 23/20-21, 35/10-11, 36/12-13, 53/1-2, etc.; (3) 78/9, 176/23, 246/6, 290/5, etc. E errs: (1) "may" for "man" 11/10, "sayde" for "onede" 79/22, "alle" for "als" 80/20, "alle" for "also" 141/12, "merueylouslye" for "mercyfullye" 149/9, "besye the" for "be seene" 230/17, "fayrenesse" for "fornece" 242/8, "renewys" for "rennys" 292/4, "besynesse" for "heuy—" 340/12; (2) 6/13-14, 22/9-10, 46/3-4, 145/1-2, 148/12-13, 181/17-18, etc.; (3) 117/15, 169/15, 182/22, 199/8, etc.

apparatus to 478/4. Another common error is seen where each scribe tries unsuccessfully to reconstruct the sense of a passage evidently badly mangled in his model: B "as twey ["wyndowys" cancelled] wyndes þat blowyn togeders breith"; E "as two wyndows þat blowen togyddere breye on eyre" 467/10-11. (The Latin versions read: "sicut duo venti insimul flantes unum aerem spirant.")

The common antecedent implied by these examples is at least one stage removed from the autograph translation. The number of intermediate stages between this ancestor and B through one branch of lineage and between it and E through another branch is unknown, but the generally good condition of both these texts argues for few if any rather than many layers of transcription. These conclusions are illustrated in the following simple stemma where X represents the Latin source, Y the autograph English translation, and Z the common parent ancestor of B and E.

B. VERSIONS OF *LIBER SPIRITUALIS GRATIAE*

The initial account, entitled *Liber Specialis Gratiae*, comprised a prologue and seven long parts subdivided into chapters. The first five parts, cataloguing Mechtild's mystical experiences, were compiled by sisters at Helfta during the last years of Mechtild's life (1241-1298). Shortly after Mechtild's death the same authors added Parts VI and VII recounting the death of Mechtild, visions in which she appeared to other nuns, and the praiseworthy life of Abbess Gertrude of the same community.

At present the most accessible text of the complete *Liber Specialis Gratiae* is the critical edition by Dom Ludwig Paquelin of the Benedictine Abbey of Solesmes[10] based on the "Guelferbytanus codex" (Wolfenbüttel) dated 1370. This version is regarded as a reliable descendant of the first record because of its antiquity, comprehensiveness, and claim of fidelity to the account then preserved at Helfta. It begins:

---

[10] *Revelationes Gertrudianae ac Mechtildianae*, 2 vols. (Paris, 1875-7), 2: 1-422. Hereafter cited as *Revelationes*.

Incipit liber specialis gratiae de sanctimoniali quadam Mechtildis nomine, quae vixit circa annum Domini MCCLXXX. in claustro dicto Helpede; quod monasterium est translatum ad civitatem Ysleiben anno Domini MCCCLVI [sic]. In die Sti Severi Episcopi primo intraverunt; et ego Albertus sacerdos eram ibi. Postquam librum istum conscripsi, et Domina Abbatissa monstravit mihi librum quem ibi habuit, et perscrutatus sum veram veritatem.[11]

As early as the mid-fourteenth century a condensation of the work was in circulation on the Continent; thereafter most copies in Latin and the vernacular manifested some degree of abridgement. The most common format included two general prologues (the result of splitting the original single prologue) and the first five parts, each a drastic reduction of its counterpart in the initial compilation. Parts VI and VII were usually omitted. These relatively compressed versions fall into separate groups differentiated by variations in textual features. The *Booke*, a five-part text, is derived[12]from a shortened *Liber*. In an effort to identify if possible the source of the English translation, the abridged *Liber* found in four manuscripts in England and in an early printed copy will be examined below. Although one of these is incomplete and two postdate the Middle English translation, each represents differences in arrangement and readings that demonstrate divergent lines of the antecedent manuscript tradition, one of which might be related to the source. It must be stressed that in the ensuing examination primary attention is not given to tracing out the relationships and descent of these texts, a procedure that would involve a detailed inspection of all the known manuscripts scattered through-out Europe, and one that is irrelevant for the present purpose.

OXFORD, BODLEIAN LIBRARY, MS TRINITY COLLEGE 32 (T)

Paper; $11^3/_{16} \times 7^3/_4$ in.; 126 folios + three flyleaves. Mid-fifteenth century. Contents: The *Vita Christi* by Ludolph the Carthusian[13] (ff. 1^{r}61^r) written in one hand in two columns of text on a page; *Liber Spiritualis Gracie* (ff. 62^r-126^r) in another hand. This text is in single columns enclosed in outlined margins, from 26 to 35 lines on a leaf; catchwords, gatherings irregular. Rubrics used liberally throughout. The *Liber* includes two prologues and five parts.

---

[11] Ibid., p. viii. The correct date for the move to Eisleben is 1346; see "Documenta" in the same volume, p. 716.

[12] The translator makes clear that he is not undertaking an independent revision of a fuller Latin account; see his own prologue (65/2-66/5) and 68/7.

[13] Ludolph died in 1377. His work was very popular in manuscript form and was printed in 1472 in Cologne.

OXFORD, BODLEIAN LIBRARY, MS DIGBY 21 (D)

Parchment; $6^3/_4 \times 4^7/_{16}$ in.; 186 folios + four flyleaves. Mid or later fifteenth century. Single columns of text ruled in ink horizontally and vertically, usually 26 lines to the page; catchwords, gatherings in eights. First folio very elaborately decorated and illuminated; ff. 73^v, 94^v, 116^v, 131^v where successive parts begin are only slightly less elaborate. Other capitals frequently ornamented, always those beginning chapters. Scroll designs around catchwords; scattered drawings of a heart, a crucifix, and pointing hands. Contents: *Liber Spiritualis Gracie* (ff. 1^r-147^r); following is an unnumbered folio and then the *Alphabetum divini amoris* (ff. 148^r-186^r) wrongly ascribed to John Gerson (f. 186^r).[14] The *Liber* has five parts prefaced by two prologues; between the prologues is a passage extracted from the work itself.

OXFORD, BODLEIAN LIBRARY, MS LAUD MISC. 353 (L)

Parchment; $9^5/_{16} \times 7^1/_8$ in.; 61 folios + one front flyleaf. Written in a mid or late fifteenth-century Contiental hand. Two columns of text, unruled, from 31 to 34 lines to a column. No catchwords or signatures, the latter probably cropped when the manuscript was rebound. Decorated capitals, some not filled in; some folios faded, some defaced by holes. Formerly part of Oxford, Bodleian Library, MS Laud 396[15] which along with several other Laud volumes was once the property of the Cistercians of Erbach, near Mainz, Germany. Their monastery was noted for its excellent library. Contents: *Liber Spiritualis Gracie* (ff. 1^r-61^r) containing two prologues and only Parts I and II, the chapters of which are unnumbered.

CAMBRIDGE, UNIVERSITY LIBRARY, MS FF. 1.19 (C)

Parchment; $8 \times 5^1/_2$ in.; 136 folios (recently refoliated) + two flyleaves in front, one in back, the last two folios blank but ruled. Written by John Whetham[16] of the London Charterhouse in 1492. One column of text ruled in red horizontally and vertically, averaging 25 lines to a page; gatherings in eights, signatures and catchwords. Illuminated initial capitals for each part;

---

[14] The author is John Nider (1380-1438), a German Dominican.

[15] Annotation in the Bodleian's copy of Henry O Coxe, *Catalogi Codicum Manuscriptorum Bibliothecae Bodleianae Partis Secundae Fasciculus Primus* (Oxford, 1858), col. 267.

[16] There is some ambiguous information that Whetham transcribed another copy of this work in 1513. See N. R. Ker, *Medieval Libraries of Great Britain*, 2nd ed. (London, 1964), p. 123. The monk was still alive in 1534 when he signed the oath of succession with some other members of the Charterhouse: Dom Lawrence Hendriks, *The London Charterhouse* (London, 1889), p. 369; see below, p. 50, item 16.

initial letters of chapters in red as are chapter headings and other decorative touches throughout. The front flyleaves contain portions of Genesis 8, 9, 10, 11 from the Vulgate Bible. Contents: *Liber Spiritualis Gracie* (ff. 1ʳ-134ᵛ) comprising two prologues separated by a short passage and then followed by the text of the five parts. The colophon is bracketed on the left by a large rubricated IHC and on the right by a rounded M (for Maria) surmounted by a crown.[17] The last line of the work reads "Trinitati laus" and is followed on the next line by the M device again.

LIBER SPIRITUALIS GRATIAE (P)

In an early sixteenth-century printed volume[18] of 202 folios, paginated 1-190 + 12 unnumbered prefatory leaves. Text of single columns averages 60 lines on a page; first gathering in twelve irregularly signatured, subsequent ones in eights. Attractively decorated with ornamented initial letters of chapters and with woodcuts of the six men and women[19] whose books and revelations are recommended for spiritual reading.[20] The *Liber* has two prologues and five parts. In his prefatory letters, the editor is vague about his sources[21] and hints that interpreters have tampered with the words of Mechtild and St. Hildegarde.

THE LATIN SOURCE OF THE *BOOKE*

i. *Structure*

In his own prologue, which precedes the two general prologues, the translator makes two points about his treatment of the Latin source (65/13-66/2): (a) he acknowledges that he has excised some material "in this begynnynge" on the grounds that it is repeated elsewhere in the work; (b) he

---

[17] This is part of the common seal of the Charterhouse. See Dugdale, *Monasticon Anglicanum*, 6: 1, 9.

[18] *Liber Trium Virorum et Trium Spiritualium Virginum*, ed. Jacobus Faber (Paris, 1513), ff. 150ᵛ-190ᵛ. The heading preceding the work is "Mechtildis Virginis Spiritvalis Gratiae Libri Primi." P will be regarded as a manuscript for purposes of textual examination. (The University Library, University of Illinois, Urbana, owns a copy of this volume.)

[19] Hermas, Uguetinus, Robert d'Uzes, St. Hildegarde of Bingen, St. Elizabeth of Schonau, and Mechtild.

[20] There were two copies of this edition in the Brigittine house at Syon: *Catalogue of the Library of Syon Monastery Isleworth*, ed. Mary Bateson (Cambridge, 1898), M107, M121.

[21] Dom Paquelin suggests that this *Liber* conforms to two Parisian manuscripts (*Revelationes*, 2: xii). E. Ph. Goldschmidt, *Medieval Texts and their First Appearance in Print* (London, 1943), pp. 53-57, describes the pioneer work done by Faber (Jacques Lefèvre d'Étaples) in publishing representative texts by mystical writers of the Middle Ages.

claims that he has followed the contents of the revelations "als thay stande in the booke." Even though all the abridged versions listed above except L show superficial structural resemblance to the *Booke*, the application of criteria implied in the translator's statements shows that C and D rather than P or T most closely conform to the source in structure.

(a) In C and D, the passage inserted between the two general prologues begins:

> Et iste liber fere totus a persona sibi familiari cui secreta reuelare consueuerat ita conscriptus est ut hec dei ancilla ignoraret.

This is nearly an exact reproduction of material that appears again in the last chapter of Part II. It also appears in L, P, T at the end of Part II but never in the prefatory section. Plainly the Latin source of the *Booke*, like C and D, included the passage in two places but the translator deleted it from his own introduction.

(b) The *Booke*'s five parts contain 87, 42, 43, 38, and 22 chapters respectively. L's unnumbered chapters amount to 72 and 44 for Parts I and II (the only parts in the manuscript), and its contents are on the whole more expanded than the translation and are frequently but not always similar to the fuller *Liber* in the critical edition S.[22] It is obvious that L's incomplete account represents a line of abridgement different from the more condensed versions of C, D, P, T. The chapters in these latter manuscripts do not consistently match each other or the translation because of occasional discrepancies in combining or dividing the contents, never because of omission or addition of material. Furthermore, except for one instance the text of the *Booke* and C, D, P, T also correspond in the arrangement of material. The significant exception concerns Part IV, chs. 18 and 19 in the *Booke*. In P they are the final chapters of Part III. In T the first portion, beginning, "Et dominus de alia ait tribus modis," is appended to Part IV, ch. 17, and the second portion, beginning "Item orabat pro una persona," starts a new chapter, Part IV, ch. 18. In C and D the passages are Part IV, chs. 18 and 19. They are thus the Latin texts that agree with the *Booke* in all particulars concerning position and division.

ii. *Readings*

This resemblance is strengthened by those readings which show the *Booke* reflecting the corrupt variants found in C and D. Sometimes the mistakes are also in P or T or both. In the following examples S shows the earlier and correct forms. (a) "euerelastyng" 208/15; CDPT "eternam"; S "internam."

---

[22] For convenience *Revelationes*, 2, will be designated by S and will be regarded as a manuscript.

(b) "sternes" (stars) 232/20; CD "sideribus"; PST "cedris." (c) "desyrede
God more preciouslye" 243/18-19; CDT "deum preciosius desiderans"; P
"deum arctius desyderans"; S "deum prae omnibus desiderans." (d) "as
companye gaderede with a fulle hastie feersnes openeys a gate or a dore"
257/12-14; CDT "ut velut conventus rapidissimo impetu januam aperit"; PS
"ut velut cum ventus rapidissimo...." (e) "þe refute of alle poure" 306/21;
CDPT "refugium omnium pauperum"; S "... peccatorum." (f) "brydde"
335/9; CDT "auis"; P "apes"; S "apis." (g) "in lykenes of a peese"
371/15; CDP "in similitudine pisi"; S "... piscis"; T "... pise." (h) "þrydde
howse" 380/8; CDT "terciam domum"; PS "totam domum." (i) "vij
articles of my godhede" 409/19; CDT "septem articulis diuinitatis mee"; PS
"... digiti tui." (j) "sauoures ... sauourynge" 572/1, 5; CDT "fragrat ...
fragrans"; PS "flagrat ... flagrans."

Further analysis reveals that when C and D differ, the *Booke* preserves the
errors recorded in C. (a) "alle here perfeccion and affeccion" 76/3-4; C
"omnisque perfectio et affectio"; D "omnisque imperfectio et defectio"; PST
"omnisque eius imperfectio." (b) "Ande thareof hitt come that myne herte
was styrrede ande mouede so faste in the crosse" 103/2-3; C "Indeque
factum est quod tam cito mouebatur in cruce"; D "... moriebatur in cruce";
PST "... moriebar in cruce." (c) "ande alle the lovynge or worscheppynge of
seyntes and ioy ande blessedhede be ordeynede atte my wille" 369/2-3; C "...
solo nutu meo ordinant"; DT "... solo meo nutu iniciantur"; P "... solo meo
nutu initiatur et a meipso incipit"; S "...solo nutu meo incitantur." (d) "This
maydene þan þoght of here owne spede as for here owne partye" 449/3-5; C
"Tunc illa sue partis memor effecta"; D "... sue partis memor defecta"; PS
"... suae paupertatis memor effecta"; T "... sue partis memor." (e) Like C the
Booke errs (363/6-7) in absorbing part of a rubric as the last sentence of the
preceding chapter.[23] (f) A final example underscores in striking fashion the
Booke's similarity to C. The pertinent passage in all the Latin texts considered
here differs from the critical edition. In S it begins: "et sono dulcisono
intonabant omnes Angeli dicentes: 'Laus aeterna tribus personis, quod
Dominus elegit te in sponsam et in filiam'. Deinde omnes Sancti...." Dom
Paquelin, the editor of S, notes that the angels' expression of praise in several
Latin manuscripts is given only in German. He quotes the St. Gall manuscript
(mid-fourteenth century): "Lobe ewig an drin Personen, das Her Dich
verkoren hat zu einer Brut und zu einer Dochter" (p. 139). He also observes

---

[23] See Note to the text. Another similarity is the *Booke*'s reproduction (331/15-332/16)
of C's elaborate directions for reciting an antiphon. Only a succinct statement is given in D, P,
S, T.

that the printed German edition of 1503 (Leipzig), which he does not cite, had misread the passage and its errors have been repeated often since.[24] The readings in D and T, however, demonstrate that the mistakes in interpreting and transcribing the German began before the sixteenth century. D's scribe writes: "et sono dulcissimo intonabant omnes angeli dicentes Regem regum loue wil an dien personen daȝ her dith hit Koren hat zu ener brut unde zu enner tothter. Deinde omnes sancti..." (f. 76ʳ). T's version is: "et sono dulcissimo intonabant omnes angeli dicentes Regem regum loue wil Ane dien personen daȝ her dith it Koren hat zu einer brut une [?] zu enner tothre. Deinde omnes sancti..." (f. 97ʳ). Both manuscripts show corruptions in changing the meaning and in introducing the "Regem regum" phrase. Furthermore, the orthographical blunders in each indicate that the present scribes and possibly their predecessors did not know German. In C the passage is an English interpolation:

> et sono dulcissimo intonabant omnes angeli dicentes Rex regum et cetera.[25] The substance off that song was þys to owre vnderstondyng: Wurschype alle seyntys þe kyng off kynges and thankyth hym whyche hath so gracyously chose þis soulle into hys spouse and douȝther. Deinde omnes sancti... (f. 69ʳ).

The vernacular wording here is duplicated verbatim in the *Booke* where it is introduced thus:

> ande alle þe aungells with a delectable sowne intunyde þis songe in duche tonge ande sayde: *Regem regum et c.* The substance of þat songe was this to oure vnderstandynge: Worschepe, alle sayntys, the kynge of kynges... (334/14-17).

The reference here to "duche tonge" could mean that the Latin source contained the German, but some explanation other than coincidence must be advanced to account for the identical phrasing in C and the *Booke*.

Since C was transcribed in 1492 it cannot be the immediate source, but it is obvious that it has descended from the source. The relationship between C and the *Booke* on the one hand and between C and D on the other can be reconciled by hypothesizing the existence of an intermediate untraced Latin

[24] Readings from L and P are not relevant to the point under discussion, but they do show changes introduced since the fourteenth century. L "... omnes angeli dicentes Regem regum et c. Deinde omnes sancti..." (f. 43ʳ). P "... omnes angeli dicentes Regem regum laudemus trinum in personis quia te in sponsam elegit et filiam. Deinde omnes Sancti..." (f. 170ᵛ).

[25] "Rex regum, Deus noster colende" identifies a sequence ascribed to Notker Balbulus (840-912), a Benedictine of St. Gall monastery. John Julian, ed., *A Dictionary of Hymnology*, 2 vols., 2nd ed. (New York, 1907), 1: 815. "Rex regum, Dei agne" is the first line of a sequence composed by the eleventh-century Benedictine monk, Hermannus Contractus (Herman the Lame), of the Abbey of Reichenau. G. Dreves, ed., *Analecta Hymnica Medii Aevi* 50 (Leipzig, 1907), pp. 311-12. Cf. Note 263/18.

text (hereafter referred to as X)[26] between D and C. This postulate assumes
the following sequence: (a) X was a copy of D or of a version related to D;
(b) X scribe acknowledged that a line in his exemplar appeared in German,
but translated into his own vernacular what he understood to be the general
meaning of the mutilated German; (c) the English author, translating from X,
described the angels singing in German and transcribed the English interpolation as it appeared in X; (d) C, a later copy of X, omitted the reference to
German but reproduced the English passage as it was written in X. This
theory, which recognizes textual correspondences noted in the foregoing
discussion, can be expressed in the following diagrammatic schemes where A
stands for the lost original *Liber* made at Helfta in the late thirteenth century.

or

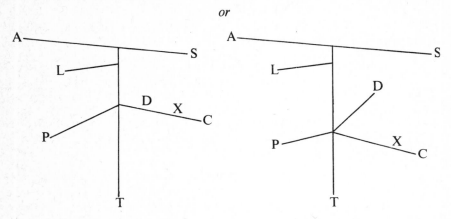

It must be acknowledged, however, that the only firm conclusion resulting
from this analysis is that C, of all the Latin texts studied, is closest in kinship
to the *Booke* and as such can be regarded as representative of the *Liber* from
which the English translation was made.

C. THE TEXT USED IN THIS EDITION

CHOICE OF MS E

The selection of either B or E for this edition could be justified. On the
whole both manuscripts are well preserved and present few textual obscurities.
Each evinces limited correction after transcription and mistakes in one can
usually be corrected by referring to the other. E is more consistently legible,
but it is about ten percent longer because its chapter headings repeat the Table

---

[26] Evidence of the existence in fifteenth-century England of untraced copies of the *Liber* is
listed below, pp. 50-52.

of Contents. B is more consistent in its language, but it has the greater number of faulty readings. Such variations as word pairs, transpositions, substitution of synonyms or dialectal forms, and additions or omissions of unimportant words account for most of the differences between the two manuscripts and of course provide no sound basis for judging either one superior. But where the variant readings are clearly scribal errors, B has more. In addition, some of B's transpositions and minor revisions distort the sense or depart from the Latin: (a) B "brouȝt me to his moder ioy," E "brought to me, his modere, ioye" (309/7-8); (b) B "badde hym to my feste," E "bade hym to my feste to eete with his brethryne" (109/18-19); (c) B "so that no cause of despeir shuld be ȝoue to hym whom folowith so moche mercy," E "so þat ... so moche mercye of þe faderes clepynge agayne" (542/3-5). Where there is no Latin counterpart, B often gives obviously incorrect readings: "merueyle" (233/9) and "compassyon" (340/20) where E has "merve-lynge" and "passyoun"; and B "y commend and betake þe to alle holy chirche," E "I betake ande commende to the alle holye chyrche" (554/4). Most noticeable are the scores of omitted single words in B and many instances of skipped fragments, not all of which are explicable by homoeo-teleuton. In sum, the more accurate copy is E. It will be the basic text, emended when the variant in B, as substantiated by the Latin source, is the superior reading.

LANGUAGE OF MS E

The following analysis of E is directed towards the identification of its dialectal character. Some of the fluctuations in phonology, morphology, and orthography are certainly due to scribal interference, but it should be remembered that it is possible that the author of the original text wrote a mixed dialect and failed to maintain a strict uniformity in transcribing sounds. An examination based on the firm criteria for dialect[27] reveals that the present text reflects—in uneven degrees—the notable features of the north and north-east Midlands.

(a) The reflex of OE *ā* (ON *á*) is predominantly non-northern *o*, but some words otherwise spelt with *o* show the specifically northern retention of the unround vowel spelt *a*(*y*), occasionally *aa*: *aane* 379/3, *aanlye, ane-* 422/15, 471/19, *fra* 126/9, 328/5, 439/14, *gaste-* 39/11, 120/19, 156/18, *hale, hayle* "whole" usually, *halye* "holy" 212/9, *hame* 32/21, *hamelye* 486/11,

---

[27] Samuel Moore, Sanford Brown Meech, and Harold Whitehall, *Middle English Dialect Characteristics and Dialect Boundaries*, University of Michigan Publications in Language and Literature, 13 (Ann Arbor, 1935); Hans Kurath, *Middle English Dictionary, Plan and Bibliography* (Ann Arbor, 1954), 8-10.

haare, hayre "hair" (alternative form *heere* from OE *hǣr, hēr*) 19/2, 3, 259/17, 18, *maste* 492/1, *mare* 351/16, 400/17, *na* 46/5, 504/4, *sare* 377/17, *stanes* 447/21, 449/11, *swa* 591/10, *twa* 57/21, 92/12, etc.; past sg. *abayde* 81/9, *rayse* 32/7, *wrate* 61/22; past part. *gane* 339/2. These *a(y)* spellings in the manuscript comprise approximately five percent of the forms derived from OE *ā* (ON *a*). Earlier *-āw* remains in the majority of spellings for "know" and "fellow" including their derivations and compounds, but OE *sāwol* is written *-au, -aw, -ou, -ow*.

(b) The loss of the second element in diphthongs *ay, oy* (where *y* represents *i* as is usual in this manuscript), well known in northern texts since the late fourteenth century, is seen in *moste* "moist" 217/12, *falleys* "fails" 213/20, *dysionede* "parted" 197/8, *ressaffe* "receive" 328/3. Conversely, *y* is used as a mark of vowel-length. Since the *y* was viewed by northern scribes as a graphic sign of length, when it appears after a vowel it has been long considered a late ME trait confined to northern areas. Such an interpretation has been challenged because *y* after long vowels has appeared in Kentish, London, and south-western works of the fifteenth and sixteenth centuries.[28] But in E alongside other indisputable dialectal usages it must be regarded as an indication of northern provenance. The present scribe never writes *-uy* for the reflex of OE *ō* nor any *-iȳyy* combination for ME *ī* and *ȳ*, but *y* after ME *ā, ē,* and *ō* is pervasive though not consistent: *boyth* 244/9, *bloyde* 116/6, *breyde* "breadth" 158/9, *choyse* "chosen" 56/11, *cloysede* 319/4, *deyde* "dead" adj. 109/16, *deyde* "death" 103/2, *heylth* 180/2, *mayde* "made" 115/10, *mayke* 124/6, *moyste* "most" 550/19, *stoyde* 239/10, *ʒoylle* "Yule" (ON *jōl*) 96/8, and the *-ay* forms cited in the preceding paragraph.

(c) OE *y̆* is most often represented by the northern and midland *y/i*. Many words are spelt also with *e*, indicating not the influence of the south-east dialect, but the unrounding of *y* to *i* and its subsequent development as ME *i*. This is verified by the numerous *e* forms of ME *i* which represent either the lowered articulation in late ME prevalent in the east Midlands or the lowered and lengthened form of OE *i* in open syllables common from an earlier period in the entire north and east.[29] In closed syllables *e* forms which might descend from OE *y̆* are *berthe* and *cherche* usually, *gerdylle* and *knette* frequently, and

---

[28] H. Kökeritz, "Dialectal Traits in Sir Thomas Wyatt's Poetry," *Franciplegius; Medieval and Linguistic Studies in Honor of Francis Peabody Magoun, Jr.* (New York and London, 1965), p. 297.

[29] Some examples of the former are *betternesse* 74/18, *geftes* 73/6, *lefte* "lifted" (<ON *lyfta*) 17/15, *melke* 207/23, *merrours* 440/9, 11, *thredde* "third" 410/16, *cresten* 60/9 unless influenced by OFr *crestien*; of the latter: *lelye* 173/17, *medille* 18/17, past part. *smetene* 234/14, *wret-* "written" 37/2, 21, 65/18 etc., *sekerlye* 458/10 (<OE *sicor*) and many inflected forms of "to give" and "to live."

others such as *beclepp-* 28/13, 93/20, *felthe* 310/20, *geltye* 424/10, *kertelle* 327/11, *kendys* 373/7, *lefte* "left hand" 6/14, 22/4, *merthe* 200/16, *threstede* "thirsted" (<OE *þyrstan* with metathesis) 356/16, *threste* 373/1 (n.) under influence of the verb. In open syllables there are *berye* "to bury" throughout; most forms of "busy" (adj. and v.) and "busily"; usually *merye* "merry," *merelye* next to *myrry* 584/5, *myrrelye* 158/22; *sterydde* "stirred" 68/13 next to *styrre* 77/15, *styrres* 106/12, *styrred* 14/19, but *sterres* 413/7. The past sg. of "to do" is mostly *dyd(d)(e)* but *dede* appears 11/14, 14/4 as well as an alternative spelling *dyede* 355/23. OE *cyssan, fyrst, byrþen* are represented by *y*, *e*, and *u(o)* spellings although *e* predominates. The rounded form is most common in the verb "to work" and its compounds (*wyr-* and *wer-* spellings are not uncommon) and in the developments of OE *mycel* and *swylc*: *moche* (*mowche* 314/2), *suche* (occasionally *swyche, swiche*). The latter also appear often in the northern spellings with retention of *l* and unpalatalized *k*: *mykelle, mykille, mek-* (with lowering), *swilke, swylke*.

(d) The typically late northern *u* for the reflex of OE *ō* is written only in *gude, gud(e)nes(se)* 327/10, 341/4, 5, 342/6, 344/21.

(e) OE *hw* is *wh*, never northern *qu* or *qw*. A few *w* spellings occur: *ware* "where" 291/20, 569/19, *wiche* 124/10.

(f) OE *sc* is represented by *sch*. Unstressed *sal(le)* for "shall," found in the north and north-east is not common: 124/6, 134/9, 228/3. Since *s* is written for *sch* so often in the north it is possible that the converse operates in *schettynge* "setting" 364/7 as it does in Rolle's *rescheyves* "receives" and Barbour's *Schir* "Sir."

(g) In personal pronouns *th-* or - forms, indigenous to the north, are almost exclusive for "their" and "them"; *here* and *hem* are fairly frequent in the early folios, thereafter rare. On the other hand, northern *scho* for "she" is rare beside the more common *sche*. Þ*ere*, distinctively northern "these," appears: 216/12, 407/8, 416/14.

(h) The verbal inflexions, though mixed, are prevailingly northern in (i) the disappearance of final *-n* in the inf. and past, pl.; (ii) *-s* endings for all persons sg. and pl. in the pres. indic.; (iii) *-e* or no inflexion when a subject pronoun for pres. indic. 1 sg. and all persons pl. precedes or follows (often this is extended to 3 sg.); (iv) the retention of final *-n* in the strong past part.; (v) *-es* forms of the imper. pl.

The work, however, abounds in exceptions to these generalizations and even exhibits northern and Midland forms side by side.[30] Midland *-ynge*,

---

[30] Juxtaposed northern and Midland inflexions of the pres. indic. are seen, e.g., 69/3-4, 76/6-7, 131/4-8, 235/24, 376/17-18, 447/13-14, 520/16.

-enge in the pres. part. far outnumbers the six northern -ande endings; -eth in 3 sg. pres. indic. is a minority form. Pres. indic. pl. of "to be" is usually be, been, bene; "are" (here written ere 116/3, 575/7 probably influenced by ON eru) of the north and north Midlands is exceptional. Most striking are several -eth endings for pres. indic. pl. and the solitary prefix y- before the weak past part. y-trauaylede 28/19, both characteristic of southern dialects.

Other significant linguistic elements and the more outstanding scribal peculiarities follow.

Vowels

OE a before a nasal not in a lengthening group is always a in "man" and "name" but naame 306/19, 20, 21 lengthened in originally open syllable. In forms for "thank" and "thankings" a and o alternate. Before lengthening clusters -ld, -mb, -nd spellings vary similarly, but hande and stande, falde and halde in both simplexes and compounds prevail. Non-northern tellyd 25/5, telde 30/8, tellede 414/13 (otherwise tolde, but talde 399/1) appear to be weak formations on the present stem.[31] Before -ng a forms are frequent exceptions: amange, emange, lange, lang(g)ere, sange (n.), strange, strangere, wranges.

ME e sometimes becomes i/y under the influences of neighboring consonants. ꝫitt occurs throughout but the following are some exceptions to the usual e spellings of the same words: brynnynge "burning" (<ON brenna), lycherye 305/14, rynne "run" (<ON renna), schydes, smyllynge, togyddere. Before supported nasals there are spryngeth (<OE sprengan "to sprinkle"), stryng(g)e(s), wynges; e and i in forms of "to think" (OE þencan) display the common confusion with OE þyncan "to seem"; the wavering in forms and derivations of "to bless" and "bliss" is familiar in ME writings.

The scribe uses y widely and usually without discrimination to designate long as well as short values of ME i and y. The combination ye (rarely ie), derived from Fr orthography and commonplace in fifteenth-century texts, is used for ME ē of various origin. This digraph alongside alternative spellings -e, -ee, -y in the same words is evidence of the sound change to [iː] in the scribe's pronunciation. Examples are here "hear" 47/21, hyere 31/12, heere 43/1, hyre 115/18; seke "seek" 48/1, syeke 162/15, seeke 487/10; also "seen" and "sick" (whose y forms may be from shortened "sickness"). Gyeve "give" probably is a new formation from OE i lowered and lengthened in dissyllabic words; similarly e and y spellings for OE lifian and sicor.

---

[31] Telde is seen in south-east Midland works of the early fifteenth century. See E. Colledge and C. Smetana, "Capgrave's Life of St. Norbert: Diction, Dialect and Spelling," Mediaeval Studies, 34 (1972), 426-7.

Less widespread is the same symbol for ME *ī*, perhaps to show the diphthong [ie] < [i:]: *fyende* 420/3, *lieche*, *lyeke* "like" adj. 3/11, 20/9, *lyefe* "life" 235/1, *plyete* 439/13, *whiet* 47/17, *wyepe* 523/14, *whyele* 262/2. The sound is written *e* in *leve* "life" 55/12 and *betynge* "biting" 442/16.

Evidence of the late ME change of earlier *-er* to *-ar* is limited: a few forms for "garnet," "heard," "hearts," and perhaps *Barnarde*. *Tarryede* "vexed" 428/19 and *terryede* 571/10 seem to show the influence of both OE *terʒan* and OFr *tarier*.

Multiple forms result from the unsystematic treatment of stressed vowels in Fr loan words: *travelle*, *traveyls* (n. "travail"); *verray* (*e*), *verre*, *verrey* (*e*) (OFr *verai*); *frewte*, *fruite*, *frute*. The stem of "to move" is spelt with both *o* and *e*, adoptions respectively from the strong and weak stems of the Fr verb.

In unstressed syllables there is great orthographic divergence. Medial *e* and *i* interchange (*beselye*, *besylye*; *bodelye*, *bodilye*); between elements in compounds or between a principal or secondary stress *e* is sometimes syncopated and sometimes not (*lef(f)ulle*, *leefe-*; *meknes*, *meke-*); and similarly with the usual ME glide between *l* and *w* in forms of "to follow" and "to hallow." An inorganic *e* is inserted between *r* + a consonant in the stems of some words: *chareges* 173/3, 5, *charechynge* "charging" 425/6, *feresenes* "fierceness" 331/2, *maretyrdome* 429/5, *peresede* "pierced" 377/19, *sterenesse* 189/2 and between the final doubled *k* in *bethenkekynge* 448/18, *thonkekynges* 445/8, *þankekynge* 394/20. ME *-el*, *-en*, *-er* are often written with *y* or *i*: *hevyne*, *mekille*, *watyre*; *a*, *o*, *u* are less frequent substitutions: *festonede* 530/11, *lechorye* 61/8, *pylare* "pillar" 256/12, *propurlye* 606/16. Among the many fluctuations in suffixes are the reduction of OFr *-iţ* to *-te* and the replacement of conventional native adjectival ending *-ouse*, *-owse* in loan words: *langores* 95/7, *meruelys* 166/9, *vertues* 179/12, 220/2, 594/7.

Some *ey*, *ie*, *ye* spellings in the final syllables of loan words suggest Fr conditions of stress: *vesseyle* 228/2, *vyrgyene* 231/3, *vigiel* 19/22, *prerogatyefe* 236/22, *saphyere* 25/17, *-iere* 273/8 (cf. *-ere* 325/5, *-ire* 273/3), but the same spellings in other syllables ordinarily unstressed in ME (*myddeyle* 220/16, *mekyelye* 244/21, *princyepalle* 594/15-16) indicate that there is no discernible rationale for the substitution of *ey* and *ye* for the more usual *e* and *i/y*. The scribe writes *y* after historically short *e* in inflexions, rarely before final *-d* and *-n* (*spreneyde* 263/14, *sodeyn* "baked" 605/3), very often before *-s*.

Consonants

Several developments have dialectal significance. For instance, besides forms of "much" and "such" noted above, there is evidence of the northern lack of palatalization of OE *c* in *ylke*, *lyeke*, *lyke*, *whylke*, *whilke*. "Church" is spelt with *ch* except when *kyrke*, common in the north and north Midlands, is used 70/12, 219/3. The unvoiced labio-dental, characteristic of the same regions, is suggested by the scattered *f* forms of parts of "to give," "to live," and "to love." The sound [v], usually written *v* initially, either *u* or *v* medially, is also *w* in *abowne* often, *Ewangeliste* 17/4, *dewels* 159/7, *meuewe-* "remind-" (from inflected OFr *muev-*) 309/3, 311/8. These *w* forms are found in northern and Scottish writings. Of interest is the excrescent *-t* after stems ending in *-gh*, *-ȝ*, *-th*, or *-wh*: *drawht*, *dreght*, *faytht-*, *feytht-*, *fertht*, *neght*, *night* "nigh," *saught* "saw," *neghtbore*, *neyȝtbore*. *Neghtbour* is found in Rolle's writings and in modern Scottish.

There might be several developments of OE final *-h*. The forms show (i) a final semi-vowel (spelt *w*, *wh*, *gh*) after both front and back vowels: *negh* (*t*), *nygh* (*t*) (OE *nēah*), *rowȝh* 573/21 and *rowhȝ* 574/3 (OE *rūh*) with scribal error for *gh*, *saugh* (*t*) (OE *seah*) whose common variant is *sawe* from pl. OE *sāwon*, *þowh*, *þowe*, *thowe* and *þorogh*, *þorow* (*e*); (ii) the reduction of the front diphthong and its combination with *-h* to form a new diphthong consistently in *hy* (*e*) (OE *hēah*); (iii) perhaps the disappearance of the back spirant in the scribe's pronunciation: *slo* 582/18, 18 (OE *slōh*, *slōg*, *slō*).

Words containing earlier *-ht* are regularly written *-ght* (*t*) or *-ȝt* (*t*). A less common spelling is *-ht*: *dowhttere* 56/10, 334/19, *fowht* 193/8, *tawht* 461/12, 463/4, 604/1, *thowhtes* 429/2, *streyhtyd* "stretched" 263/8. *Rygh* "right" 145/9 and *ryde* 243/5 are exceptional, but the latter, along with *streyte* "straight" adj. 90/2, *þowt* 226/7, *nootede* 357/10, shows gradual loss of the spirantal element before *-t* and is corroborated by the insertion of an inorganic *ȝ* or *gh* before final *-t* in *defawȝttes* 494/1, *dowȝtes* 29/10, *lyȝt* (OE *lȳt*) 485/18, *owȝt* "out" 338/1, 12, *whight* "white" 90/6.

The scribe's *ȝ* denotes both *ȝ* and *z*. It is transcribed *z* in this edition where etymology suggests that the sound value is [s] or [z]: medially in spellings for "Nazareth" and "baptized," and initially only in *ze(e)le* "ardor." In most instances it is an alternative to the more usual final *-s* in inflexions, a feature conspicuous in the northerly *Sir Gawain and the Green Knight*, the *Alliterative Morte Arthure* and Barbour's *The Bruce*, but also seen occasionally in Midland works. In this text *z* appears mainly after stems ending in *-t* and in nouns more often than verbs: (n.) *aduersiteez*, *contricionz*, *dignyteez*, *gyftez*; (v.) *fyghttez*, *forgettez*, *imaginez*. The final consonant in suffixes *-a(u)nce* and *-ence* in nouns of Fr origin is often written *-z* or *-cz*, generally only in the second half of the manuscript. This is an adaptation of the OFr usage designating the sound [ts] which was later simplified to [s]: *habunda(u)ncz*, *continenz*, *obediencz*, etc. Multiple spellings for the same word, e.g., *obediens*, *-ence*, *-encz*; *pacience*, *-encz*, *-ens*, *-enz*; and *suffyciencz*,

-*entz*, indicate that *c*, *cz*, *s*, *z*, and even *tz* all represent the sound. Such orthographic variability in writing *c* and *t* in these suffixes is perhaps behind the substitution of conventional adj. and n. endings -*ent* and -*ance*/-*ence* for each other in (adj.) *neglygence* 75/4, *reuerence* 122/4, *habunda*(*u*)*ntz* 361/5, 455/15, *obedyence* 296/16; (n.) *reuerente* 470/2. Confusion in deciphering and writing *c* and *t* is a well-known scribal error; it is curious that in E the interchange is limited to these words.

Doubling or dropping of consonants is erratic. There is a tendency to double final -*g*, -*k*, -*t*, especially before inflexions (*drynkkys*, *gattys*, *parttede*, *ryngges*). Weak verb endings in -*edde*, -*ydde* are frequent; and there are some unusual -*esse*, -*ysse* inflexions in nouns (*Crystesse* 173/16, *crommysse* 500/18, *delytesse* 135/5) and in verbs (*begynnesse* 96/13, *commesse* 479/16, *demysse* 113/14, *havesse* 24/9; note too *wasse* 108/6, 120/3, etc.). Sometimes the initial aspirate is wrongly inserted as in *hadde* 134/15, *ham* 203/7, *hopenynge* 508/6, *howre* 22/5; in words of Latin origin it is retained or omitted at will: *habyte*, *abbytte*; *hooste*, *ooste*. Occasionally *g* and *d* are dropped in the environment of *n*: *spreneyde* 263/14 (OE *sprengan*), *reynynge* "reigning" 102/2, *Wennesdaye* 31/7; similarly the *l* in *wordlye* "worldly" and the final *b* in "comb." Sporadically, a *p* develops between *m*-*n* or *m*-*t*; sometimes a *b* is seen between *m*-*r* and after *m*. A phonetic *t* is introduced once in *grutchynges* 424/14, an inorganic one in *lestene* "lessen" (v.) 465/2.

Inflexions

Nouns are generally inflected in the usual -*es*, -*ys* pattern. Gen. for titles, relationships, proper names, and miscellaneous other nouns (*maydene*, *neghtbore*) are often uninflected in the sg.; sometimes also in the pl. of "man" and "sister." "Brothers" and "children" end in -*en*; they also appear as *brethere*, *bredere*, childre(*e*), *childyr*, *childere*, the regular northern and north Midland forms used by non-northern writers as well. Several pl. forms without -*s* occur besides those used in conjunction with numerals: e.g., *conuersacion* 19/15-16, *breste* 43/10, *sepulcre* 59/14.

In adj. the addition of -*s* to the pl., based on the Fr model, is seen twice: *dyuerses* 349/7, *certayns* 555/6.

Verbal inflexions of the weak past tense and past part. are often dropped after stems ending in -*p* or -*t*.

Vocabulary

In addition to those lexical items already noted there are others associated with the northern dialects.[32] Some are specifically northern or Scottish:

---

[32] Information on currency and etymology is listed in MED (through "metal") and OED.

cledde, ouereallew hare, slokenede, sterne "star," *stye* "ladder," *syen, w hat kynne, ʒowuthede*; some are predominantly northern, north Midland, or north eastern: *egges, kyste, pappes, slyke, strekynge, titter(e)*; some are common in the north but not confined to it: *atte* "that," *dede, deyde* "death," *fra, ylke, tylle* prep. "to."

Conclusion

The work is basically consistent with a region that contained characteristics of more than one dialect. It might be contended that Norfolk is the locale since autograph works there of the mid and later fifteenth century show individual authors writing *hem, here* alongside *them, þere*, and using *-eth* as well as *-s*.[33] But Norfolk can be ruled out on the basis of the proportional incidence of these dialect features. In E the overwhelming majority of 3 pl. personal pronouns and pres. indic. 3 sg. are northerly. The relatively rare *hem* and *-eth* might be acceptable variants; certainly they are such in some Lincolnshire documents dated 1450-65.[34] Most important is the writing of *a* and *o* for OE *ā*, strong evidence alone that the manuscript was written in the north Midlands, not East Anglia. The mixture of other predominantly northern and north Midland features, the absence of significant westernisms, the random influence of Scandinavian cognates, occasional dialect words—none rare and collectively not numerous—point to an area in Lincolnshire, somewhere not close to the western boundary of the north-east Midlands and not in the midst of the preponderantly Scandinavian regions along the coast. In view of the known activity of the English and Continental Carthusians in disseminating the revelations,[35] the cautious suggestion is offered that this copy might have been written in the Carthusian house in Axholme, located in Lincolnshire near the Yorkshire border. In this connection it should be recalled that the notations on the flyleaf of the manuscript offer possible but not conclusive proof of ownership in Yorkshire between 1471-85.

The coexistence of some scattered forms definitely more south than central in mid-fifteenth century (*-eth* in 3 pl. pres. indic.; the single use of the prefix with the past part.) and the change in some forms through the text of E (as the occurrence of non-northern *here* and *hem* frequent in the early folios, and the

---

[33] See Mark Eccles, "*Ludus Coventriae* Lincoln or Norfolk?" *Medium Aevum*, 40 (1971), 136.

[34] *Lincoln Diocese Documents, 1450-1544*, Andrew Clark, ed. (EETS 149, 1914), pp. 294, 318.

[35] See below, pp. 50-51, items 15 and 16.

spellings *-z* or *-cz* only in the second half of the manuscript) suggest that the scribe of E was consciously tampering with the dialect of his master copy.

Several language developments seen in varying degrees show that the work was not written late in the century. The spelling of *ie* for ME *ē* is frequent; the shift in the pronunciation of earlier *-er* to *-ar* (apparently begun in the fourteenth century) is less common; and there is one example of the change of OE *d* between a vowel and vocalic *-r* to ME *th* (*thithere* 381/4), a spelling well established by the sixteenth century but later than the pronunciation it reflects. The evidence offers nothing more definite than the probability that E was copied around mid-century.

NOTE ON MANUSCRIPT B

This manuscript is predominantly east Midland in its linguistic characteristics, with some features suggesting the influence of a dialect more south than central. In contrast to E it maintains a high degree of consistency in adoption of forms: e.g., *brenne*, *renne*, and *syster* and derivations are regular throughout; the same is true of *meue* "move" and *preue* "prove" from the strong stems of the OFr pres. sg.

Vowels

The reflex of OE *ā* is regularly written *o*, *oo*. The Anglian form *a* lengthened before *-ld*, *-ng* is also *o* (exception *hanggynge* 159/16) but before *-nd*, *-mb* several *a* spellings appear: *handys*, *stande*, *lambe*. Before a nasal not in a lengthening group *a* is usual in "man" and "name" but *a* and *o* alternate in forms for "to thank." Sometimes *a* becomes *ai* before [ʃ] in forms for "to wash."

Examples of ME *e* raised to *i/y* before liquids and *-ng* are *-silf*, *-sylf* very often, *swyrde* 137/20, *spryng-* 147/17, *hynge* "hanged" 160/2 etc. The opposite tendency—to lower ME *i* to *e*—is seen frequently: *besy-*, *bese-* consistently, *euelle* 508/18, *lemys* "limbs" 354/16, *left* "lifted" 32/7, *peler* "pillar" 21/7, *pety* 210/4, *reuers* 8/4 and others.

The reflex of OE *ȳ* is *y* or *i* most often, but forms in *e* are abundant: usually in forms of OE *styrian*, also *dede* past pl. "did" 292/19, *gerte* 90/4, 91/8, *knett* 371/1, *merth* 402/2, *mery* 360/14 etc. Multiple forms in *y*, *e*, and *o/u* appear for "burden"; note also *kuttynge* (OE *cyttan) 604/13. OE *mycel* and *swylc* are *suche*, *moche*, *muche*, once *mochal* 346/6.

In unstressed syllables *-el*, *-en*, *-er* the vowel is commonly *e*, but in these and other syllables including inflexions and suffixes there are occasional substitutions: *myddule* 7/16, *lyttule* 12/6, *apostelus* (pl.) 15/6, *Petur* 34/1, *lengur* 70/22, *byttour* 177/4, *profitabulle* 492/8. The *u* spellings are south-west as well as north-west elements but they are of slight significance in the total work.

Consonants

The reflex of OE palatal *c* in final position is often retained: *childliche* 553/17, *liche* 3/11, 28/8, 74/20 etc., *oonliche* 11/16, *worthlyche* 92/2 etc. OE *sc* [ʃ] as well as medial OFr *s* are represented by both (*s*)*sh* and *sch*: *shalle*, *englissh*, *flesch*, *obeischaunt*. *Frenchip* 164/14 is unusual. OFr *g* [dz] is *ch* in *charch-* 331/4, *ache* "age" 261/3 and *k* in *abrekynge* "abridging" 394/4. Final *-nk* is expressed by *-ng* in *þinge* 492/20. In "negligence" and "negligent" *nec-* and *neg-* alternate for the first syllable.

Earlier *-ht* is regularly *-ʒt*, *-ght*. The loss of the fricative before *t* is implied by the spellings *not* 375/11, 378/22, *streyte* "straightened" 165/10, *wrouthe* "wrought" 36/18 and by the inorganic *ʒ* in *douʒtes* 29/10, *abowʒte* 21/6, and *slowʒþe* 440/21.

Initial OE *hw* appears as *wh* except for *wer-* "where" 297/20, 21, 312/16. Spellings of *wh* for *w* are *whas* "was" 154/10, *where* "were" 8/3.

Inflexions

In 3 sg. and pl. personal pronouns *she* and *they*, *þey* are consistent nom.; in 3 pl. possess. *here*, *hyre* and oblique *hem* are regular although *þere*, *þeire*, *them* occur a few times.

In verbs, inf. are usually without final *-n*. The common ending for pres. indic. 3 sg. is *-th*, never *-s*; sometimes no inflexion after a pronoun. Forms for "to be" are *is*, *ys* in 3 sg., *be(e)n*, occasionally *beth*, in pl. Pres. indic. pl. ends in *-e*, *-n*; less often *-th*. Imper. pl. is *-th* or uninflected. Pres. part. is *-ynge*. The past indic. pl. of weak and anomalous verbs often has final *-n*: *weren*, *seyden*, *cryden*, *seruyden*, *helpeden*, *diden*, *wenten*. Many stems of weak verbs ending in *-d*, *-t*, or consonant groups are uninflected in the past and past part.: *departe* 53/17, *deuyd* 270/19, *hurte or infecte* 185/6, *lett* 59/20, *left* "lifted" 32/7 etc. In the past part. the prefix *y-* is written a few times. In strong verbs past pl. and past part. are usually endingless.

Vocabulary

Words and forms noted in E's vocabulary are here replaced by ones of non-northern currency: *cheste* 177/15, *cloþed* 144/20, *eyren* "eggs" 603/3, *qwenchyd* 228/15, *sythen* 153/9, *souner* 375/14, 17, *sterre* "ladder" 266/5, *sterres* "stars" 232/20, *strecch-* 496/11, *suche* 66/17, *tetys* 100/9. Non-northern *dethe*, *eche*, *from*, *that*, *to* are consistent. E's dialectal *ouereallewhare* 603/11 is altered; *what kynne* does not appear; and *ʒowuthede* is *iuuent* 86/3, *ʒouth* 262/13. The manuscript chooses words and forms of OE or romance origin in contrast to those in E showing direct or indirect Scandinavian influence: *deseruen* (E *adelle*) 501/4; *almes* (E *almuse*, *allmus* < OI *olmusa*) 527/5, 565/6; *aschyn* (E *askes*) 74/20; *biclipp-*, *beclipp-* (E *hals-*) 26/16, 387/6, 9, 10, 12; *held-* (E *hell-*) "pour" 283/1; *helth* (E *heyle*, ON *heill*) 95/16, 98/22 etc.; *hang-* (E *hyngg-*, OI *hengja*) 159/16; *swaged* (E *sawhtelde*, *saghthelde*, LOE *seht*, *saeht*, ON *saht-r*) 121/2, 7. *Stappes* "steps" (n.) 156/7, 396/18 is found in southern writers, influenced by the v. WS *staeppan* (OED "step" v.). Of interest is *bredyth* 158/9 (elsewhere *brede*) a late formation first recorded in the fifteenth century.

Conclusion

Traces of northern antecedence survive in *awher* 487/13 (OE *ā + hwǣr*), possibly in *ligge* "lie down" 604/18 (which is either a derivation from ON *liggja* or a single example of the southern development of OE *cg*), and in *ar* "before" 62/10 which might be from OE *ǣr* or **ār* rather than ON *ár*. To be noted too are the few northerly forms in the other works in the manuscript: pres. indic. 3 sg. *byddes* fol. 102^r/35, *eetis* fol. 102^v/26, pl. *preysys* fol. 101^v/12, and *behalde*, *mykelle* fol. 101^v/11, 19, all of which seem to show the present scribe or his predecessor altering originally northern texts.

The almost pure east-Midland character is affected by the scattered southern features (*beth* for "are," many pres. indic. pl. in *-th*, past part. with *y-*) and points to a locale more south than central. The admixture of such elements along with a sprinkling of westernisms is characteristic of London English in the 1450s, seen for example in Pecock's *Folewer to the Donet*,[36] c. 1454, but there is nothing persuasive to connect B with the London area. The scribe's association with the London Charterhouse[37] is at best conjectural. The date is also imprecise. Watermarks, tentatively identified, hint at the possibility of the third quarter of the century, but the almost exclusive use of *here* "their" and *hem* "them" in this copy suggests a period closer to 1450 since the *th-* spellings were majority forms in London English after mid-century.

THE *BOOKE* AS TRANSLATION

It is possible to make some generalizations about the *Booke* as translation even while acknowledging that E is not the autograph copy and displays some amount of scribal alteration. To the extent that the translator neither rearranges nor omits anything, he fulfills his pledge to present the matter as it

---

[36] E. V. Hitchcock, ed. (EETS 164, 1924).
[37] See above, p. 2, n. 4.

stands in the book. Full-scale interpolations are insignificant in the whole, being restricted to a rare expression of personal reaction (75/21), a sentence or two for transitional purposes (191/6-9, 476/4-6), the endorsement of a hymn (97/7-13), an invented reply (481/15-17), the substitution of a pious exercise for those who cannot recite a recommended Latin prayer (539/2-9), and a mild protest about the orthodoxy of one passage (567/8-12). Other additions are minor, usually repetitions and incidental ideas embedded in sentences. Furthermore the *Booke*, always faithful to the *Liber* in emotional coloring and didactic intent, also preserves its variety of discourse which comprises instructional exposition, dramatic narrative, and visionary description. Assorted forms of dialogue including interrogations, exhortations, imperatives, and apostrophes are likewise duplicated.

But no simple generalization describes the English author's inconsistent method and the uneven quality of his prose. He vacillates from strict conformity to free paraphrase, from controlled and clear expression to inept and confused phrasing. In some cases he closely follows the *Liber* right down to details of syntax and diction with only slight adjustments to accommodate English idiom:

> In hoc verbo laudem qualiter deus laudat se in seipso laude perfecta sine fine.
>
> Ande furste be this worde, *laudem*, sche hadde knowynge howe God worscheppede hymselfe in hymselfe be a perfytte worscheppe withowtene ende (77/10-12).
>
> Angeli et archangeli suo obsequio faciebant ut omnes qui aderant michi maxima in reuerencia et deuotione seruirent.
>
> Aungels ande archaungels mynystrede me be þare seruyse þat alle þo þat were aboute me servede me in fulle grete reuerence ande deuocioun (239/19-21).

At the other extreme he arbitrarily follows his own bent, ignoring the sense of his model and substituting his own thought:

> Throni conquesti sunt quod pacatissimum regem eorum qui thronum in ea firmauerat sepe inutilibus cogitacionibus inquietando turbasset.
>
> Thronys mayde playnte ande sayde þat fulle ofte sche was trublede ande dysqwyete inasmoche as in here was with vnprofytable þowȝttez þat peesable kynge whiche hadde sette in here a throne of stabylnesse ande of dyscrecion ȝif sche wolde haffe holdene hit (169/7-11).
>
> Et ipsi tota gratitudine sua dulcissima fruicione refluunt in ipsum.
>
> Ande þaye with al þare gladdelye herte torneys agayne into hym with a fulle holye abydynge with hym ande onelye for hym (292/6-8).

It must be granted that his work maintains an overall adherence to the form and content of the Latin model but ranges in degrees of adaptations in parts of the individual sentences.

Close translation does not guarantee accuracy. The *Booke* often gives exact English equivalents of Latin misreadings: "lybertey" (171/22) "libertas"; "presence" (370/7) "presencie"; "partyes" (448/9) "partibus." Such errors confirm the use of a corrupt *Liber* and cannot of course be charged to the translator. Similarly other senseless phrases might be attributable to disjunction ("inuita" becomes "in here lyffe" 298/14) or conjunction ("in gratitudine" is given as "of here vnkyndenesse" 525/1) in the Latin copy, but "herde fruyte" (352/17) for "dulcissimum fructum," "his prayer" (456/6) for "racionem," "wyne ... in this cuppe" (82/21) for "poculum uiuum," "euerelastynge dignite" (122/9-10) for "eterne diuinitatis" show the translator's carelessness or his mechanical response to Latin mistakes. Either explanation indicates that his habit in these examples is to work in small units in disregard of the larger context. This uncritical procedure is seen again in the following excerpt where "quasi" is an interpolation and "redacta" should read "redactus": "... in cuius aspectu mellifluo quasi cinis ad nichilum est redacta." Unmindful of the similitude just expressed (74/20) likening Mechtild's clothing to ashes, the translator strains to stay close to the corrupt Latin: "... ande with that delectabylle syght sche felle into noȝt fro hereselfe als brennede woode tornede to askes" (75/18-19).

In the light of his disposition to be cavalier elsewhere none of this is evidence of the translator's slavish devotion to his source. When he is alert to confusion in the Latin account he does not hesitate to interfere with the text, but his imaginative contributions are often more confusing than clarifying. For example, at the end of a chapter (481/12-17) the *Booke* follows the text of the incorrect *Liber* which quotes Mechtild asking a question of Christ. (In the correct version the chapter ends after Christ, not Mechtild, asks a rhetorical question.) The translator, evidently dissatisfied with the *Liber*'s conclusion that offers no reply to Mechtild's query, invents a perplexing statement that purports to be an answer: "Als þowȝ sche hadde aunswerde hereselfe ande sayde: 'None hevynesse maye abyde in suche a sowlle'" (481/15-17). Again, where the *Liber* has "mundam" instead of "nondum," the English version patches together a reading that loses sight of the metaphorical use of "security" ("pignus") established earlier.

Sicut rex, qui sponsam suam mundam perduxit in domum suam, urbem aut ciuitatem aliquam diuicijs plenam amicis suis in pignus exponit....

Ande ryght als a kynge þat haffes brought his clene spows into his howse or into a cite fulle of rychesses, he puttys here þare for luffe ande in tokene of luffe emange his frendys... (547/13-16).

And in a section already badly disorganized in the abridged *Liber* (see Note for 586/3-4), the translator worsens matters first by confusing speaker and listener and then by altering the sense of the question:

> Et dixit domino: quid te coegit ut michi indignissime et uilissime talia conferres.
>
> Þan sayde owre lorde to here: "Whate compellede the þat þou schulde speke in thyne herte so vnworthylye ande lowlye to me ?" (586/12-14).

Most of his other changes, however, are not amendments of a faulty text; even where all versions of the *Liber* are correct and unambiguous, he is inclined to tinker with small phrases: "Virtutes, in cumulum honoris mei..."; "Vertues, whiche were kepers ande the hye cause of mye worschepe..." (239/17-18).

This freedom in handling his source is the English author's way of carrying out his ideas on purpose and policy as announced in his incipit and explicit. To the audience of religious who could not read the *Liber* he declares that (a) his work is meant for their "comforth ande techynge" (65/9) and "encres of deuocion or of oþer gostelye grace" (612/17-18), and (b) his intention is to translate "playnlye withoute curiouse termes to ȝour vnderstandynge" (612/15-16). In practice he neither expounds nor clarifies in any meaningful sense but restates and amplifies in an effort to increase the already richly edifying content and affective phraseology of the *Liber*.

The alterations are never discourses of any length, merely expansions of parts of sentences and additions of bits and pieces. A single Latin word is rendered as a string of synonyms: "inhumaniter" "vngoodelye, dyspitouslye, ande greuoslye" (425/8-9); or as a clause: "Et sicut cervus" "Ande ryght as þe beste whiche es callede a herte" (300/8-9). A passing reference becomes a repetitious summary: "in medio suprascripte coree" "in the myddele of þat companye of virgyns whiche were so knette togedders to oure lorde with a threfolde corde as itt es sayde before" (278/17-19); specific terms are substituted for less precise ones and minor details are added: "ad conuiuium meum" "to my feste to eete" (109/18-19); "circumdata" "werene ledde abowte in suche a karolynge" (274/9). Doublets, all-pervasive and often tautological, include many from the stock supply ("answerede ande sayde," "worscheppede ande thankkede," "heyle ande saluacioun," "ioye ande blisse") as well as others inspired by the Latin: "inuitare" "to clepe ande styrre" (77/14-15); "pedegogum" "kepere ande gouernere" (80/8); "dei faciem" "the faace or the syght of God" (88/18); "album sacculum" "a white pooke or a litylle white sakke" (388/9-10). Some function as frankly pious tags: "pro hijs" "for these ande alle othere gyftez ande gracez" (152/15-16); "ab omnibus maculis" "of alle fylþes ande spottes of synne" (329/19); "insidias inimicis" "priuey aspyes or þe false suggestions offe the enmye, the fende" (302/1-2).

Other tendencies work to slacken even more the unhurried pace of the *Liber*. For the Latinless audience there is a translation of every Latin phrase: "*Accipite iocunditatem glorie vestre*; þat is to saye: Takkys þe myrth off ʒowre blysse" (402/1-2). Another device, helpful to readers and listeners but tediously prolix, is the painstaking enumeration of each item in a series, as in the following excerpt from nine greetings to the Virgin:

> Saluta, inquit, uirgineum cor.... Humilimum.... Deuotissimum.... Quarto feruentissimum....
>
> Thowe schalte salute furste þat herte of virginite.... The secounde gretynge schalle be þat þowe schalte salute here herte whiche was moste meke.... The thrydde gretynge schal be that þowe schalte salute here herte whiche was moste deuoute.... The ferthe gretynge schalle be that þou schalte salute here herte whiche was moste feruent... (85/6-20).

Changes in similitudes are invariably expansions, either by elaboration:

> Sed ego tanquam filio suo mater illis obuiam ueni ut eos de faucibus luporum eruerem.
>
> Botte I come ande mette with þame as a tendere luffynge modere metys with here sonne to save hym fro perels. Ande so mette I with þame for I wolde delyuere þame fro þe wolffys mowthes (164/16-20).

or substitution:

> ... quia castigacio carnis redolet ante deum ut thymiama suauitatis.
>
> For chastysynge of the flesche gyffes a swete sauour vppe to oure lorde, as a swete confeccioun made of dyuers spyces gyffeys a swete sauour to a mannys smelle (124/1-4).

or invention:

> melliflue diuinitatis gazophylacium
>
> þe tresoure of þe swete godhede þat passis alle the swetnesse of any honye (329/8-9).
>
> ... ita ut audiret et sentiret pulsum cordis eius
>
> ... insomoche þat sche herde ande felte of his herte þe powse betynge lyke to a powse of a strange mannes arme (102/15-16).

Gratuitous doctrinal commentary inevitably lengthens the English sentence which sometimes wanders off into a syntactical jungle.

> Quia quanto homo sanctior est coram deo tanto se reputet inferiorem omnibus et uiliorem et quo mundior est consciencia a peccato eo plus timet et precauet ne dei incurrat offensionem.

Ande that was no wondere for the holyere that a mane be in the syght of God,
the lowere & vnworthyere he schulde have hymselfe, ande preferre al oþere
abowne hymselfe. Ande the more clerere a man felys his owne conscience or
clene fro synne, the more he awe to drede in awntere he hadde offendede God
whareby he was blyndede that he cowthe nought knawe hymselfe, or els drede
his infirmite that be his awne frelte he myght or schulde ryght sone falle (75/7-
14).

But even when not cluttered by extraneous insertions, the loose constructions
of the English sentences often depart from the Latin system of modification
and subordination.

Viditque ipsam beatissimam trinitatem, in similitudine fontis viui ex seipso sine
inicio existentis, et in se omnia continentis, qui mira amenitate effluens et tamen
in se indeficiens permanens irrigabat et fructificare faciebat vniuersa.

Ande þare sche sawe þe blyssede trynyte in lykenes of a qwyke or leuynge welle,
whiche was of hymselfe withowten anye begynnynge ande conteynede alle
thyngges in hymselfe whiche schewede owte hymselfe with a wounderfulle
gladnes and ȝit in hymselfe he dwellede ande aboyde stylle contynuelye ande
nowȝt fayllede, ande moystede alle thynges & made þaim bryngge furth frewte
(229/15-22).

This drift, however, along with the arbitrariness in shifting from precise to
approximate meanings, is suspended in certain heightened portions such as
those incorporating solemn pronouncements by Christ or fervent prayers.
These sections are stylized in expression and somewhat formal in structure,
though in fact most are a series of brief statements with a minimum of
complex subordination. The English author customarily adheres to the Latin,
duplicating clausal patterns and retaining (and even extending on a modest
scale) verbal ornamentation.

Benedicat te omnipotencia mea. Instruat te mea sapiencia. Repleat te mea
dulcedo. Attrahat te et vniat mecum mea benignitas sine fine.

Myne myght þat es allemyghttye blesse the. Myne wysdome informe the. Myne
swetnes fulfylle the. Ande myne benignyte drawe the to me ande oone the with
me withowtynne ende (104/17-20).

Ecce do tibi aurum, id est diuinum amorem meum. Et thus, id est omnem
sanctitatem et deuocionem meam. Et mirram, id est amaritudinem tocius
passionis mee.

Loo, I gyffe the golde, þat es to say my luffe of the godhede. I gyffe the encense,
þat es to saye alle holynesse ande my deuocioun. Ande I gyffe the myrre, that es
to saye the bytternesse of my passioun (117/5-8).

An extended prayer (191/10-194/6) comprising five long aspirations owes
its entire design of balance, repetition, and interlocking refrain to the *Liber*.

These and other passages demonstrate the translator's ability to imitate or invent simple stylistic devices. It therefore seems unaccountable when he is indifferent to touches like parallelism and climactic gradation that should have been transferred to the English rendition for clarity and force.

> ... scilicet ut mundas habeant cogitaciones, sancta desideria, dulcia inuicem verba, et caritatiua opera.

> ... þat es to saye, þat þay haffe clene þoughtes, holye desyres, clene wordes in comwnynge of gostelye swetenesse, ande in excercyse of werkes of charyte (251/5-8).

> Feruentissima ... summa in pietate ... prima in humilitate et afflictione ad semet-ipsam.

> Tharefore sche was fulle fervente in charyte ande deuocion, ande fulle hye in pyte ande besynes to here evene cristene, ande sche was desirous in mekenesse ande afflyccion of hereselfe (610/4-7).

He is more consistently sensitive to the advantage of variety in the normal sentence order. Inversions of basic sentence elements are frequent: "a softe herte ande a pacyente" (103/7), "hitt es gastelye woundede ande heylfullye" (156/18-19), "no worschepe desyrynge ne bodylye commodyte" (217/9-10). This impulse is not geared for any special effect other than the avoidance of monotony, as is seen in the following: "Sche lovede wele pouerte, ande grete feruour hadde ande deuocion, & abovene alle thynge moste sche profytede in charyte to God ande to man, for seruyseable ande amyabylle sche was..." (72/10-13). Occasionally ambiguities occur as when coordinate elements such as "ryche" and "plenteuous" in the first example below and "blasphemez" and "accusacions" in the second are too far apart: "makys ryche alle lyuelye thyngges ande plenteuous" (132/11-12), "whate blasphemez for luffe of my spowse in þe stede of merye songe ande false accusacions my eeres herde" (411/4-5); or when modifiers are misplaced: "an harpe come owte fro the deuyne herte whiche hadde many strengys" (334/9-10), "ande with þe eere of his herte intentelye sche lystenede" (326/8-9).

Alliteration is a favorite but not an overly conspicuous device, sometimes suggested by the Latin:

> Hec est speciosior sole et sideribus sublimior.

> Þis sawle es more speciouse þan the sunne ande hyere þan þe sternes (232/19-20).

sometimes independently achieved:

> ... infra te quoque firmamentum tenens animam tuam.

Ande withynne the I schalle be a sykere schettynge holdynge stabbylye þy sowlle ... (364/6-8).

One long section (113/12-114/5) is unusual. It contains seventeen alliterations on *d*; the Latin equivalent has six inflexions of "judicare." The excessive alliteration here is an extreme instance, but in other respects the passage is a fair example of the translation at its best: it transfers the exact meaning, it inserts a minimum of extra phrases, and—most important—it is clear and orderly because it stays close to the guiding constructions of the *Liber*.

2

The Revelations of Mechtild of Hackeborn

A. THE COMMUNITY AT HELFTA: ITS SPIRITUALITY AND CELEBRATED MEMBERS

The convent at Helfta[1] in Saxony was originally founded in 1229 in Mansfeld by Burchard, count of Mansfeld, as a Cistercian monastery,[2] but was moved by the count's widow in 1234 to more suitable surroundings in Rodardsdorf. It was to the latter place that Gertrude, daughter of Baron von Hackeborn, came at an early age. She was elected abbess there in 1251 when she was nineteen years old; in 1258 she moved the community to Helfta, about a mile outside Eisleben, where larger quarters had been donated by her two brothers. Here the monastery remained for almost ninety years,[3] a period when it was known throughout Germany as a house of piety and learning.

During the thirteenth century the country was astir with unsettling events and attitudes: conflicts between the papacy and German and French thrones, moral laxity among clergy and laity, and recurrent famines, plagues, and wars. Simultaneously, and perhaps even partially as a consequence of these disorders, a vital religious spirit emerged. It found expression in increased vocations not only to the older established religious orders, but also to the new

---

[1] The prefaces to *Revelationes*, 1 and 2, provide information on the cloister at Helfta and the lives of St. Gertrude and the two Mechtilds. "Documenta" (ibid., 2: 713-731) reprints material concerning the history and personnel of the monastery. For additional material on Helfta, see Lina Eckenstein, *Woman Under Monasticism* (Cambridge, 1896), pp. 328-53; A. Mary Robinson, *The End of the Middle Ages* (London, 1889), pp. 45-72; Dom Gilbert Dolan, o.s.b., *St. Gertrude the Great*, 2nd ed. (London, 1925), pp. 1-7; and Sister Mary Jeremy, o.p., *Scholars and Mystics* (Chicago, 1962), pp. 1-30.

[2] The community was never incorporated into the Cistercian Order, since the year before its foundation the General Chapter had refused to accept any new convents. However, the nuns at Helfta kept the Cistercian Rule and wore the grey habit. By the mid-fourteenth century records refer to them as Benedictine, and so they passed over to Benedictine affiliation. See *Revelationes*, 2: 713-14, and Gabriel Ledos, *Sainte Gertrude* (Paris, 1901), pp. 8-10.

[3] It was shifted once again in 1346 to another location called New Helfta, inside the walls of Eisleben. Nearly two centuries later the cloister was ransacked and destroyed during the Lutheran reform.

foundations of Dominicans and Franciscans whose energetic preaching and evangelical piety were powerfully attractive. Religious houses, especially of Dominicans, sprang up everywhere in Germany. Educated women in the cloistered life also had a part in the new movement. Convents of nuns proliferated[4] and, under the instruction of spiritual directors and through study and meditation, many of them became centers of religious culture.[5] But monastic life did not draw all devout Christians. Those who remained in the world found it possible to develop an interior piety by joining small informal communities of beguines or their less numerous but equally active male counterparts, beghards.[6] Another sign of the new religious enthusiasm was the expression of fervent and personal love. The minnesingers had cultivated this impulse in their chivalric songs to nature, lord, and lady. Now religious poets—Mechtild of Magdeburg and Henry Suso are outstanding ones—in their vernacular writings transformed the lyrical style of the courtly suitor into outpourings of reverent devotion. In the midst of this ferment and still strongly linked to the past through the Benedictine Order, Helfta prospered under the forty-year enlightened rule of Abbess Gertrude von Hackeborn (d. 1291).

Intelligent, devout, and an able administrator, the abbess fostered high intellectual and spiritual standards. Within the convent manuscripts were collected and transcribed; the nuns were educated in theology, Scripture, and the liberal arts; and mysticism thrived. Here the richly talented St. Gertrude the Great (1256-1301 or 1302) came as a child in 1261, and developed into a learned and holy religious.[7] She edited and translated Latin manuscripts, composed numerous prayers, compiled the *Spiritual Exercises*, and wrote the second book of *The Herald of Divine Love*, the record of her own revelations

[4] In 1287 there were 70 Dominican convents in Germany and 18 in all the other provinces combined: Jeanne Ancelet-Hustache, *Master Eckhart and the Rhineland Mystics*, trans. Hilda Graef (New York, 1957), pp. 19-21.

[5] It has been suggested that the remarkable development of the mystic spirit in the fourteenth century is in some sense related to the influence of scholastic philosophy on the spiritual lives of these highly educated women. Eckhart, Tauler, and Suso preached at convents. See James M. Clark, *The Great German Mystics* (Oxford, 1949), p. 5; David Knowles, *The English Mystical Tradition* (New York, 1961), p. 34.

[6] These lay people devoted themselves to charitable works and the pursuit of Christian perfection. Mostly unlettered and under no firm spiritual guidance, both beguines and beghards later came into disrepute as a result of tendencies towards a vague heretical mystical pantheism. Robert E. Lerner, *The Heresy of the Free Spirit in the Later Middle Ages* (Berkeley, 1972), pp. 35-181, alludes to the persecutions launched against these controversial people.

[7] An old error, perpetrated in devotional manuals and religious art especially, assumed that Abbess Gertrude and St. Gertrude were the same person.

and visions.[8] Her extant works show a knowledge of the writings of St. Augustine, St. Gregory the Great, St. Bernard, and Hugh of St. Victor. It was Helfta too that Dominican directors selected as a haven for the elderly beguine Mechtild of Magdeburg (d. 1282 ?).[9] This mystic, whose unfinished lyrical work circulated in her own lifetime, had earned the active dislike of certain clerics and laymen for her outspoken criticism of their scandalous conduct. At the monastery where the poet-visionary was cordially received about 1270,[10] she completed Book VII of her mystical experiences recounted in *The Flowing Light of the Godhead*. In the same cloister Mechtild of Hackeborn, younger sister of Abbess Gertrude, learned and gifted in her own right though less scholarly than St. Gertrude and less literary than Mechtild of Magdeburg, received the special graces described in *The Booke of Gostlye Grace*.

These women lived at the threshold of the Golden Age of German mysticism. The full flowering occurred in the fourteenth century when, under the impulse of scholastic teaching and inspired by the Neoplatonic strains inherited from the Victorine and Dominican commentators, the spiritual giants of the Rhineland and the Low Countries effected "a remarkable, perhaps a unique, phenomenon in the history of mediaeval culture." [11] Eckhart (d. 1329 ?), Tauler (d. 1361), Suso (d. 1366), and Ruysbroek (d. 1381) represent that vigorous mysticism at once theoretical and practical which combined the love of philosophical speculation with the ethical and devotional demands of a perfected Christian life.[12]

The mysticism at Helfta was only slightly touched by the currents of the new movements. It was almost wholly molded by the older Benedictine school and is marked by the distinctive accents of St. Bernard's spirituality. The tradition is exemplified in the writings of a number of pious women. In Germany the prophetical and evangelical tracts of the Benedictines, St. Hildegarde of Bingen (d. 1179) and St. Elizabeth of Schonau (d. 1164),

---

[8] From the sixteenth century on, the *Herald* has been edited and reprinted several times. The *Exercises*, less well known, was translated in *The Exercises of Saint Gertrude*, ed. A Benedictine Nun of Regina Laudis (Westminster, Md., 1956).

[9] Usually referred to as Sister Mechtild, she has never inspired an active cult. Her contemporary fame, her influence on St. Gertrude and Mechtild of Hackeborn, and her genius have been explored in studies of mysticism. See, e.g., Jeanne Ancelet-Hustache, *Mechtilde de Magdebourg (1207-82), Étude de psychologie religieuse* (Paris, 1926).

[10] Her chronology is uncertain; see ibid., p. 44 et seq., and *The Revelations of Mechthild of Magdeburg (1210-1297) or The Flowing Light of the Godhead*, trans. Lucy Menzies (London, 1953), p. xx.

[11] J. M. Clark, *The Great German Mystics*, p. 1.

[12] Jean Chuzeville, *Les Mystiques allemands du XIIIe au XIXe siècle* (Paris, 1935), pp. 17-18.

echoed St. Bernard's preaching on the need for spiritual renewal and clerical reform. Later in the Low Countries, the spiritual diaries and biographies of the Cistercians, Ida of Nivelles (d. 1231), St. Lutgarde (d. 1246), Beatrice of Nazareth (d. 1268), Blessed Ida of Louvain (d. 1300), and the mysterious beguine Hadewijch (d. 1269 ?), all show the impassioned fervor of the Bernardine doctrine of love.[13] This spirit, with its vivid expression of intense emotion, eventually characterized the thirteenth-century Benedictine temper.[14] At Helfta the affective strain predominated, despite the impressive theological training reflected in St. Gertrude's *Spiritual Exercises* and evidence of contemporary Dominican thought in Mechtild of Magdeburg's *Flowing Light of the Godhead.*

Few specific biographical facts about Mechtild of Hackeborn are recorded in the *Booke* and must be supplemented by material in *The Herald of Divine Love* by St. Gertrude, in the surviving registers of the convent, and in the fuller *Liber*. She was born into the noble Thuringian family of Hackeborn, probably in 1241. When she was seven years old, she petitioned so eagerly that permission was granted for her to join the nuns at Rodardsdorf. Later she moved with the community to Helfta. In effect she was an assistant to her sister the abbess in administrating the affairs of the monastery although her special duties were to direct the choir, train young novices, and teach in the convent school.

In the course of performing her assigned offices she became first the mentor, later the cherished companion and confidante of St. Gertrude. Numerous comments throughout the unabridged *Liber* call attention to the beauty of Mechtild's singing[15]—hence the title *domna cantrix*[16]—and to the tender concern and pious example she displayed as a teacher. Her devotion, amiability, and compassion were outstanding even in the saintly community at Helfta. The final chapter of the *Booke* sums up these and other testimonies to her virtue. She died after a long illness in 1298 or 1299. Although her name

[13] The writings of the last two women point the way to a speculative mysticism. See Stephanus Axters, o.p., *The Spirituality of the Old Low Countries*, trans. Donald Attwater (London, 1954), pp. 20-24, and Sister M. Columba Hart, o.s.b., "Hadewijch of Brabant," *The American Benedictine Review* 13 (March, 1962), 1-24.

[14] Axters, *The Spirituality of the Old Low Countries*, pp. 16-18.

[15] Wilhelm Preger, *Geschichte der deutschen Mystik im Mittelalter*, 3 vols. (Leipzig, 1874-93), 1: 83-86, sees two persons in Mechtild the chantress and Mechtild the sister of the abbess. His argument is based on the surname of Wippra given to the chantress in the old documents. The name, however, belongs to the Hackeborn family; see Ledos, *Sainte Gertrude*, p. 16, n. 3, and Jeremy, *Scholars and Mystics*, p. 32.

[16] Dolan, *St. Gertrude the Great*, p. 11 n. She is also called the Nightingale of the Lord.

is not listed in the Roman martyrology, her cult is approved, and her feast day is kept in some Benedictine monasteries on 26 February or 16 November.

Mechtild's life was not marked by any great spiritual "conversion" as was St. Gertrude's nor was she subjected to the hostility that Mechtild of Magdeburg encountered. Unusually free from the obstacles of overwhelming doubts and temptations, her path to sanctity was strewn with other sufferings, such as severe physical afflictions and a tormenting conviction of her own imperfection. Nevertheless, it is not sorrow but love that sounds the prevailing note in her visions, a love that expresses affection for her fellow creatures and worship of the Godhead. In her fiftieth year (1291), during a period when she was seriously ill and Abbess Gertrude was dying, she recounted in confidence some of her visions to two companions. The *Booke* tells us that many more she would not describe: "Also itt was sometyme so spyritualle þat sche sawe þat be no waye sche cowth ne myght nouȝt schewe itt in wordes" (407/12-14). Her companions privately recorded her experiences for the next eight years, but at some point Mechtild became aware of their secret labors and was disconsolate. The *Booke* relates that in her distress she complained to Christ, who reassured her that the written record was part of his providential plan to make known his special favors; moreover he gave the work its title and promised to guide the writers and shower blessings on those who were edified by the account (406/13-407/7, 586/21-587/15).

The consensus is that St. Gertrude was undoubtedly the principal compiler and, because of her ill health, was assisted by another nun.[17] St. Gertrude's own revelations mention Mechtild frequently, and some visions therein also appear in Mechtild's account. But there is no reference to Gertrude in the *Liber*, a surprising fact in view of their close friendship. Furthermore the *Liber* claims that the piety of Mechtild had never been matched by anyone in the monastery (603/8-11); yet at the very time St. Gertrude's reputation for remarkable sanctity was well known, even outside Helfta. These apparent slights are attributed to St. Gertrude's humility and deliberate silence regarding her own spiritual life.

B. THE ABRIDGED *LIBER*: CONTENTS AND FEATURES

The streamlined five-part *Liber* is the work of an editor who acknowledged the tediousness of the initial cumbersome account. In the last chapter of his abridgement (closely translated in the *Booke*) he remarks that the "schewynges" listed should suffice, adding that the "notabylites" left out are

---

[17] The evidence is reviewed in *Revelationes*, 1: xv-xviii.

of very great number: "botte nowe we make þe ende þat þis booke schulde nowʒt torne into werynesse to þe reders, whiche God wille nouʒt, for þe lenght ne for þe multiplyenge of maters" (600/7-9). His version reduced the encyclopedic sweep and repetitive elements by compressing the first five parts and omitting the sixth and seventh parts.[18] His method of abbreviating the parts was to discard some chapters entirely, to shorten others by excising beginnings or ends, and to create new ones by combining fragments from two or more chapters of the original. By trimming the lavish details the reviser has shaped a more manageable *Liber*, but his alterations are sometimes disjointed and abortive, usually because he has arbitrarily excluded parts of the larger relevant context.[19] Despite these lapses there is a general unity of structure in that the opening and final chapters, comprising a brief factual introduction and an elaborately laudatory conclusion to Mechtild's life, enclose five parts that still conform to the orderly divisions first determined by the authors at Helfta and described in the second prologue (68/3-21).

Part I, which amounts to more than half of the *Booke*, is arranged around the seasons and holydays of the liturgical year. Part II lists the special graces bestowed on Mechtild. Part III gives guidance for "the helthe of manys sawle." These instructions are continued in Part IV with specific direction to religious men and women. In Part V, the briefest section, visions of dead persons show how the deceased depend on the prayers and good works of the living.

The selection of material from the fuller *Liber* was clearly determined by the editor's intention to concentrate on the teaching content. Most of the visions he extracted are those connected with the liturgy as recognized and observed in the universal Church: standard feasts, the Divine Office, the Sacraments, the Mass. These and the less numerous but equally splendid visions associated with Mechtild's personal piety are always followed by an appropriate meditation and a moral discourse. Details of Mechtild's history and the activities of the Helfta community are usually ignored.[20] The new *Liber* with its focus on the homiletic features buried in the longer account is less a celebration of Mechtild's sanctity and more a compendium of formulae for intensifying devotional feelings.

Both long and short versions were geared from the outset to a specific

---

[18] A small amount of material was shifted to new positions in the abridgement: some sections of chs. 8, 9, 13 in Part I became chs. 39, 40, 41 in Part II; some sentences from Part VI were transferred to the end of Part V (see Notes for 607/3-21, 610/4-611/4).

[19] See, e.g., Notes for 381/4-10, 509/15-510/8, 586/3-4.

[20] Exceptions, such as the reference to the interdict placed on the monastery and the vision of the deceased founder, are obviously justified because of the pious morals appended to the incidents.

audience: all of Part iv and admonitions scattered elsewhere about obedience to superiors, attentive recitation of the Office, and spirited singing in the choir are applicable only to religious. The work's suitability for those in cloistered life is noted in the English author's remarks to the "sustrene" (65/13 and 612/13) who requested the translation.

The *Booke* is not a guide to the interior life teaching the ascent to the heights of contemplation, nor is it a speculative analysis of any system of mystical thought. It is, furthermore, wholly devoid of the reforming zeal, prophetic warnings, and anti-heretical polemics so common in the works of other women mystics. Its non-theoretical orientation concentrates on the ordinary means of pleasing God. The stages of the mystic way receive no methodical treatment, but the *Booke* states repeatedly that Mechtild's union with God was the climax of a sustained life of prayer and self-discipline. Its strong recommendation of ascetic practices shows the influence of St. Bernard's teaching, especially in injunctions to humility, obedience, and resignation to God's will, and in frequent reminders that spiritual trans-formation is a lifelong struggle. Penitential exercises and private devotions are explicitly approved but, in accordance with the standard of Benedictine piety, the *Booke* gives primacy of importance and attention to common prayer in the canonical office and the conventual Mass.[21] Like that of St. Gertrude and the earlier Cistercian, St. Lutgarde, Mechtild's mysticism is steeped in the Opus Dei. This is manifested in the visions and revelations of Part i, a calendar of the church year. Prayers, antiphons, hymns, responses, psalms, gospels, everything that constitutes the liturgy of the ecclesiastical cycle fosters her meditations and stirs her imagination, yielding scenes and dialogues for elaborate spectacles wherein she is sometimes an active participant and sometimes an awed witness. Phrases chanted in choir inspire many of the visions of the other parts too; private devotions and data from the lives of the saints also function as stimuli, but on a smaller scale.

The allegorical nature of the revelations is also fundamentally simple and uncomplicated, but always vivid and colorful. As is to be expected, most of the pictorial representations reflect the medieval symbolistic conception of the universe which sought to discover the truly significant realities beneath the actual appearance of an object or the literal sense of a writing. Such a view was formed by centuries of biblical exegesis that had focused on the allegorical, moral, and anagogical interpretations,[22] and, since the twelfth century,

---

[21] Pierre Pourrat, *Christian Spirituality*, 3 vols., vol. 2, trans. S. P. Jacques (London, 1924), 1-2.
[22] See Beryl Smalley, *The Study of the Bible in the Middle Ages* (Oxford, 1941).

pseudo-Dionysian thought that regarded visible phenomena "mystically," that is, as symbolic of virtue or vice or some idea of the Word that had to be discovered.[23] It should be emphasized, however, that the distinctive ideas and nomenclature of pseudo-Dionysian mysticism as systematized and taught at St. Victor are not descernible in the *Booke*. Mechtild's visions are cluttered with items whose deeper meanings are stated precisely: a fair tree, beasts and men under its branches and birds flying above are respectively the Church, souls of men, and devils (158/7-159/11); the lily and the rose on Christ's shield represent his innocence and patience (173/17-18); silver is cleanness of heart, gold is love (177/18-20); the trefoils and shields on Christ's clothing figure the Trinity and the victory of the Resurrection (188/18-189/6). Certain details represent divine teachings: the placing of the Cross in the sepulchre symbolizes Christ's promise to bury himself in her (166/18-167/4); and the host in its gold box suggests the mystery of the Eucharist hidden from the knowledge of men and angels (254/12-17). In all this there is no effort to fathom the divine mysteries at all; Mechtild's account shows no trace of a philosophical scheme that attempts to render theological science both speculative and affective.

Symbolic numbers, popular in every branch of medieval thought from theology to science, are also prominent in the *Booke*. The Church had inherited from St. Augustine and his predecessors the recognition that number theory—once the original pagan number mystery had been pressed into the service of religion—was an important key to cosmic secrets.[24] Following the meditations on the One in the greatly influential pseudo-Dionysian tract *On the Divine Names*, medieval mystics accepted number as the most exact symbol for the Unknowable, and proceeded to find evidence of significant numbers throughout the universe. In scriptural exegesis, in sermons, in church architecture and ritual, numbers were interpreted for their ultimate relationships.[25] The essentially mysterious character of numerology appealed

---

[23] Pourrat, *Christian Spirituality*, 2: 110; pp. 108-29 give a survey of the spirituality of the school at St. Victor where elements of Greek Christian thought, inherited from pseudo-Dionysian writings, exerted some influence.

[24] See Vincent Foster Hopper, *Medieval Number Symbolism* (New York, 1938). Since Patristic times theologians had attempted to establish the numerical relationship of the supramundane, the ecclesiastical, and temporal worlds. For example, starting from the arche-typical numbers three and four as symbols respectively of the divine and earthly spheres, the combination of both came to represent the spiritual and temporal duality of mankind. Thus the seven gifts of the Holy Spirit, the seven Beatitudes, and the seven petitions of the Pater took on impressive connotations of the essential harmony and totality of all things. (Ibid., pp. 82-86.)

[25] See Mary Anita Ewer, *A Survey of Mystical Symbolism* (London, 1933), pp. 104-12.

especially to creative writers. The imaginative descriptions of Mechtild's visions use numbers in this traditional sense, naturally as a mode of expression and very much alive with meaning. Undoubtedly at times numbers merely suggest convenient limits, but most usages designate definite symbolic intentions. Three, which connotes the Trinity, is most frequent: a threefold cord springs from Christ's heart, there are three knots in a garland, one worships God three ways in His saints, and a recommended devotion calls for the recitation of three Aves. Five, usually symbolic of the flesh because of its association with the five senses, is another favorite: Mechtild adores the Five Wounds, God promises five rewards to his friends, and a soul should seek Christ in five ways.

Added to this already heavily symbolic cast of the *Booke* is the recourse to symbol in recording the visions, voices and dramatic dialogues that often accompanied Mechtild's contemplative and ecstatic states. Such psycho-physical phenomena, merely accidental accessories[26] to the highest reaches of the interior life, might be considered the artistic expressions and creative results of the mystic's intuition of God's presence in her soul "... combining with material supplied by a poetic imagination, and expressing itself in an allegorical form." [27] It is only in terms of a language of the spiritual senses, applicable by analogy, that the mystic can reconstruct what is essentially intellectual and non-corporeal.[28] Mechtild's articulation of the mystic experience in terms of physical sensation is consistent with her temperament. The more striking revelations combine colorful scenes and lively dramatic dialogues and are accompanied by elaborate explanations that can be classified loosely into two categories. The first identifies those discourses that clarify some doctrinal matter or incite the soul to more fervent devotion. They are associated with symbolic panoramas, appearances of the saints and the Blessed Virgin, and visual depictions of events in the life of Christ. Here Mechtild is taught the meaning and consequence of the Incarnation; she is instructed in the types, counterfeits, and rewards of virtues; she is directed to the proper disposition for receiving graces and the Sacraments; and she is shown the hideous punishments for a heedless and selfish life. The revelations of the second group are of a more personal nature. There is a certain amount of explicit spiritual guidance, but the emphasis is on the magnificent pageantry of the celestial courts and the bliss of intimate concord with God.

---

[26] Cuthbert Butler deplores the tendency to equate these concomitants with mysticism: *Western Mysticism*, 2nd ed. with *Afterthoughts* (London, 1951), p. lviii.

[27] Evelyn Underhill, *Mysticism* (New York, 1955), p. 286; see also pp. 125-48, 266-97.

[28] A. Poulain, s.j., *The Graces of Interior Prayer*, trans. from 6th ed. by Leonora L. Yorke Smith (London, 1912), pp. 88-113.

Both groups testify to Mechtild's imaginative and emotional sensitivity. She delights in noting the stunning colors and designs of robes, the sparkling rays of precious stones and metals, the merriment in heaven, the organ-like sounds of angelic choirs, the heartbeats of Christ, the softness of silk, the fragrance of incense, and the savoury draughts of spiritual refreshment. Stately processions, flowing rivers, carols of angels, whirling gold discs in the Virgin's clothing, and St. Agnes censing the convent add movement and sound to the brilliance of the ornately wrought pictures. In the midst of these splendours, Mechtild is in turn frightened, curious, fascinated, and amazed. She is tender at the Nativity, grief-stricken at the Passion, exultant at the Resurrection, sorrowful for her own faults, and compassionate towards sinners.

Commentators have observed that romantic vernacular poetry affected the quality of mysticism at Helfta.[29] Clearly the elements of lyric song in the service of mystic love were familiar to the nuns through the presence of Mechtild of Magdeburg, but it is very likely that the same nuns brought from their aristocratic homes some knowledge of the minnesong. Thuringia was celebrated as one of the chief resorts of the knightly poets whose courtly songs reflected, in part at least, the pervasive effects of the Provençal troubador lyrics.[30] Chivalric overtones, characteristic of current secular poetry, were adapted by Mechtild in the revelations. Pictures of court life abound: shields and escutcheons are described, the principal figures wear majestic robes, Christ sits on a throne, the Blessed Virgin is crowned with a diadem, angels bear banners in regal processions, and Christ appears as a knight.

By far the greatest number of images are those common to medieval mystical literature. The personification of virtues, especially Love, is a standard device. The appearance of the soul as a vineyard and as a foul garment, Christ as a gardener, the Blessed Virgin as a fair tree, the Holy Ghost as an eagle, the Trinity as a well, and the face of God as a sunbeam are stock comparisons. Some of the more complex designs function as symbols of spiritual progress. The mountain of seven degrees leads the gradually purified soul to the throne of God (143/3-145/10); the ladder of nine steps arranges souls and angels in a parallel hierarchy (266/5-269/17); the four houses on the great hill are suitable heavenly abodes for souls in different stages of spiritual perfection (404/7-405/16); and the hours of the Divine Office

[29] Menzies, *Mechthild of Magdeburg*, p. i; Evelyn Underhill, "Medieval Mysticism," *Cambridge Medieval History*, 7 (1932), 797.

[30] See Margaret Fitzgerald Richey, ed., *Medieval German Lyrics* (Edinburgh, 1958), pp. 9-29.

represent the successive steps from purgation to union (469/11-471/3). The descriptions of the ecstatic state of union with God use familiar similes: the wax and seal, birds in the air, fish in the sea, a drop of water and the ocean, iron and fire, wood burned to ashes, and melted gold. One important feature of this state, though neither unique nor original with Mechtild,[31] is the culmination of the love and nuptial symbolism in the mystic espousals. Since the time of Origen expositions on the Canticle of Canticles had expressed the craving of the soul for its perfect mate in the language of human love.[32] Just prior to Mechtild's own time Bernard's sermons on the Canticles and Richard of St. Victor's *Four Degrees of Passionate Love* had expounded on the fulfillment of the Bride-Soul's yearning for the Bridegroom-Word in terms of marriage imagery. The *Booke* too expresses the ardent soul's relationship with her Lord in the phrases of bridal passion. Mechtild and Christ's exchange of rings (409/3-15) symbolizes the mystical union of wills, but not necessarily mystical marriage or perfect transforming union.[33] The exchange is a spiritual betrothal, a pledge of that complete cleaving or oneness with God that remains to be ultimately effected in the highest stages of union.

Prevailing spiritual currents helped shape the *Booke*'s enthusiasm for certain devotions, notably those to the Virgin and to the humanity of Christ. Although other mystics had preached and written on these cults,[34] St. Bernard's sermons contributed most significantly to their popularity. Mechtild followed the line of Bernardine piety which extolled Mary's humility, holy virginity, and divine maternity. Some of her more rhapsodic visions are inspired by Mary's role as gentle mediatrix and heavenly queen. The focus on the mysteries of the earthly life of Christ was characteristic of medieval spirituality generally but was vigorously promoted by St. Bernard as the necessary means of approaching God. Although the object of the highest mystical contemplation is the Christ-God, in which images of the Sacred Humanity no longer form a part, meditations on the circumstances of Christ's life are effective stimulants for animating and intensifying spiritual fervor in the initial stages of purgative preparation. Mechtild, like St. Bernard, is partial to the Nativity and the Passion. The infant, the manger, the swaddling clothes, the name of Jesus, the Circumcision, the sufferings and humiliations of the Crucifixion, the repentance of Mary Magdalene, each touches her heart

---

[31] St. Lutgarde and St. Gertrude participated in the spiritual espousals.

[32] Butler, *Western Mysticism, Afterthoughts*, p. 110. A brief history of the treatment of the Canticles appears in "The Interpretation of the Song of Songs," by H. H. Rowley in *The Servant of the Lord and Other Essays on the Old Testament*, 2nd ed., rev. (Oxford, 1965), pp. 197-245.

[33] Poulain, *The Graces of Interior Prayer*, pp. 283-91, explains the distinction.

[34] See Félix Vernet, *La Spiritualité médiévale* (Paris, 1929), pp. 77-92.

and overwhelms her with the love of Christ for men and awakens in her a corresponding love.

After the time of St. Bernard, attention was directed to specific features of Christ's humanity, particularly the wounds of the Passion, and soon replaced the earlier but more impersonal veneration of the Cross.[35] In the twelfth century the devotion to the Five Wounds of the crucified Christ was just barely acknowledged. By the thirteenth century it was matter for private piety and it figures in the writings of Mechtild and St. Gertrude.[36] Special concentration on one of the Wounds, that of the Side, assures Mechtild an important place in discussions on the nature, meaning, and development of the Sacred Heart cult. The custom of honoring the human heart of Christ beating in His glorified body was publicly and officially recognized in 1673, when the Church accepted as authentic the visions of St. Margaret Mary. In one sense varying blends of the veneration can be traced back to the early ages of the Church but the devotion to the Sacred Heart as it is understood today had its roots in the medieval devotion to the Wounded Side.[37] The transition took place probably in the thirteenth century, although some historians see unmistakable signs in the twelfth.[38] Certainly the cult exists in embryonic form in *Vitis Mystica*,[39] and St. Lutgarde had a vision of the pierced Heart of Jesus. In the revelations of St. Gertrude and St. Mechtild it is a full-fledged devotion complete with a multitude of exercises and showerings of special graces.[40] Mechtild rests on the Sacred Heart; she hears the Heart beating;

[35] Louis Gougaud, *Dévotions et pratiques ascétiques du moyen âge* (Maredsous, 1925), p. 79.

[36] Douglas Gray, in tracing the popularity of the veneration, makes several references to the revelations of Mechtild and St. Gertrude: "The Five Wounds of Our Lord," *Notes and Queries*, 208 (1963), 50-51, 82-89, 127-34, 163-8. See Note to 220/17.

[37] See J. Bainvel, "Cœur sacré de Jésus," *Dictionnaire de théologie catholique*, 3, 1 (1938), cols. 271-351 for a history.

[38] Rev. Arthur R. McGratty, *The Sacred Heart Yesterday and Today* (New York, 1951), pp. 25-26.

[39] A tract once ascribed to St. Bernard, later to St. Bonaventure, now acknowledged to be of German origin, either from Franciscan or Cistercian circles; see *Heart of the Saviour: A Symposium on Devotion to the Sacred Heart*, ed. Josef Stierli, trans. Paul Andrews, s.j. (New York, 1958), p. 69.

[40] As the original title, *Liber Specialis Gratiae*, indicates, the graces are special to Mechtild; St. Margaret Mary's visions announced universal graces. The devotion was very active during the fourteenth century and appears to have been concentrated almost exclusively in Germany, where the Dominicans are credited with organizing a complete asceticism around the mystery of the Sacred Heart. In the next two centuries the Carthusians became the most active promoters; the monks at the Cologne Charterhouse were responsible for making the texts of the medieval German mystics accessible, and early engravings at the Grande Chartreuse show an attachment to the cult. See *Ancient Devotions to the Sacred Heart of Jesus*, Carthusian Monks of the XIV-XVII Centuries, 4th ed. (London, 1953), pp. viii-ix; and *Medieval Devotions to the Sacred Heart*, ed. Karl Richstatter, s.j. (London, 1925), pp. 6, 38-39, 141-8.

Christ draws her soul into his Heart; he gives his Heart as a pledge and as a house of refuge. These familiar relations represent a simple and tender phase of the development of the cult. Christ's Heart shows itself loved and triumphant; it is not the suffering Heart of St. Margaret Mary's visions. To St. Mechtild, the Heart is an overflowing fountain of redemptive graces.

Mechtild's import is not confined to religious annals. She figures in literary history as well because she has been mentioned in the unresolved controversy concerning the identification of the lovely Donna Matelda in Dante's *Divine Comedy*. Since scholars are agreed that the poet habitually drew his allegorical characters from real life, they have diligently hunted for the prototype of the maiden who greets travelers at the entrance to the Earthly Paradise.[41] She is meant to represent a type of temporal felicity, perhaps "... love rightly ordered and inflamed by divine inspiration; awaiting the mystical ascent to the vision and fruition of God." [42] Some commentators have seen in Mechtild the original of Matelda.[43]

Copies of the *Liber* were rapidly disseminated after its completion in the late thirteenth century. Dom Paquelin's edition describes thirteen extant manuscripts in Latin and the vernacular languages located in libraries on the Continent.[44] Another Latin copy[45] should be added to that list. There is a Dutch version in the Bodleian Library.[46] An untraced version either in Latin or Dutch is included among the 109 volumes entered in the surviving catalogue of the Franciscan Tertiaries at Delft.[47] Printed versions date from a 1503 German text; by 1605 there were 14 editions in Latin, German, French, Italian, and Spanish. Most of these are not complete and many appear in conjunction with the visions of St. Gertrude.[48] No English edition has been printed from either the long or short *Liber*, although an English translation of an earlier digest in Latin was published in 1875.[49] Countless works on

---

[41] The lady appears first in the *Purgatorio*, 28, 40 and is mentioned by name in *Purgatorio*, 33, 119.

[42] Edmund G. Gardner, *Dante and the Mystics* (London, 1913), p. 270.

[43] See Note for 143/3.

[44] *Revelationes*, 2, viii-xi.

[45] Described in Francis Halkin, "Catalogus codicum hagiographicorum latinorum Paderbornensium et Osnabrugensium," *Analecta Bollandiana*, 55 (1937), 239-40.

[46] MS Douce 44. See F. Maddan, *Summary Catalogue*, 4: 502.

[47] See Margaret Deanesly, *The Lollard Bible and Other Medieval Biblical Versions* (Cambridge, 1920), p. 115 n.

[48] Dom Ursmer Berlière, *La dévotion au Sacré-Cœur dans l'Ordre de s. Benoit* (Paris, 1923), pp. 40-53, has a survey of printed editions through 1922 which in some respects supplements Dom Paquelin's list (*Revelationes*, 2: xi-xv). One not noted is *Revelationes Selectae S. Mechthildis*, Bibliotheca Mystica et Ascetica, vol. 10 (Cologne, 1854).

[49] It is a translation of the Cologne edition; see preceding note.

Mechtild have been compiled in English as well as in other vernacular
tongues, but they are devotional manuals for the most part and are derived
only remotely from the earlier revelations.[50]

[50] For example: *The Love of the Sacred Heart, Illustrated by St. Mechtilde* (London, 1922);
and *O Beata Trinitas, The Prayers of St. Gertrude and St. Mechtilde*, trans. Rev. John Gray
(London, 1927).

3

The Revelations in England

A. EVIDENCE OF CIRCULATION AND POPULARITY

The extant manuscript copies of the *Booke* and the *Liber* have already been noted. A number of other fifteenth-century documents contain passages in Latin and English[1] pertaining to the revelations. These references are here grouped and itemized under three headings identifying the general nature of the documents: compilations of mystical writings, devotional works, other records.

Compilations of Mystical Writings

(1) *London, British Library, MS Sloane 982* is called *Extracta de libris Revelationum Dei Beate Birgitte.*[2] Ff. 54ʳ-61ᵛ describe a series of visions in Latin (one brief English passage appears on f. 60ᵛ) from the works of Mechtild and St. Birgitta.[3] Most of the material on Mechtild is adapted from Part ɪ, ch. 18, in the unabridged *Liber.*[4] F. 133ᵛ has a fragment in English attributed to "Molde" beginning: "Here followes an askynge of our lordes blessynge."[5]

(2) *London, British Library, MS Harley 4012* contains fourteen entries of devotional material all in English.[6] The fourth (ff. 77ᵛ-78ʳ) begins: "Theis be the wordis that oure saueoure Ihesu spake to his holy spouse and virgen Sent Moll. In al thi werkis kepe iij thingis in thi mynde."[7] This manuscript has

---

[1] None of the selections in English correspond verbatim to the *Booke*.

[2] Edward J. L. Scott, *Index to the Sloane Manuscripts in the British Museum* (London, 1904), p. 347.

[3] The folio marked 57 is misplaced. The English passage on f. 60ᵛ is listed in Jolliffe, *Check-List*, item I. 7 (a).

[4] *Revelationes* 2: 51-60. Cf. *Booke*, 160/21-180/2.

[5] Cf. *Booke*, 517/16-18.

[6] *A Catalogue of the Harleian Manuscripts in the British Museum*, 4 vols. (London, 1808-12), 3: 103-104.

[7] Cf. 436/17-437/6. Listed in Jolliffe, *Check-List*, item I. 31 (b).

connections with Syon and Sheen: the ninth item is "The Pardon of the Monastery of Shene which is Syon."

(3) *London, British Library, MS Lansdowne 379* is a Book of Hours.[8] At the end of a section, possibly of Carthusian origin, on the revelation of the Hundred Pater Nosters there is an account of the efficacy of the devotion (ff. 52^v-53^r). The writer mentions the practice of a Mount Grace Carthusian of adding a prayer before reciting each hundred Paters "whiche litel prayer the holy virgyn saint Mawde vsed to say thus in latyn." The prayer is short, beginning: "Domine Ihesu Christe filii dei viui suscipe hanc orationem," and is followed by a close English translation.[9]

(4) *Cambridge, University Library, MS Dd.xiv.26* has nine divisions, the third of which is a series of paragraphs in Latin and English, in prose and verse, on religious topics.[10] After a prayer to SS. Kateryne and Margarete, item lx (ff. 45^r-46^r) begins: "Owre lorde God seyd to Seynt Mawde his blessyd virgyne & holy spowse." Then follow paraphrases of Christ's counsels to Mechtild on conduct becoming his "dere doȝter," on proper devotion to the holy wounds, and on efficacious prayers for the dead.[11]

(5) *Cambridge, Peterhouse, MS 276* belonged originally to the Carthusian Charterhouse of St. Anne, Coventry. It is described as a Psalter although 16 folios of prayers and devotions in Latin and English precede the Psalter.[12] On ff. 6^v-7^r are three Latin prayers identified as coming from Mechtild's revelations;[13] they are followed by a prayer from St. Birgitta's revelations.

(6) *Cambridge, King's College, MS 18* is titled *S. Ambrosii Quaedam.*[14] On the last folio (104^v) is a list of seven books which Peter, vicar of Swine (Yorkshire), gave to the Cistercian house of nuns there in the first half of the century. Among the volumes is the Latin account of the revelations.

(7) An untitled manuscript in Downside Abbey,[15] catalogued as *Prickyng*

---

[8] *A Catalogue of the Lansdowne Manuscripts in the British Museum* (London, 1819), p. 110.

[9] The *Booke* gives the entire prayer in Latin, but merely summarizes its intention in English (538/20-539/9). The devotion is discussed by Francis Wormald, "The Revelation of the Hundred Pater Nosters," *Laudate*, 14 (1936), 165-182.

[10] *A Catalogue of the Manuscripts Preserved in the Library of the University of Cambridge*, 5 vols. (Cambridge, 1856-67), 1: 530.

[11] Cf. 531/10-16, 538/5-10, 539/2-9, 581/13-20, 428/21-429/6, 381/20-382/5. The extract is listed in Jolliffe, *Check-List*, item I. 31 (a).

[12] M. R. James, *A Descriptive Catalogue of the Manuscripts in the Library of Peterhouse* (Cambridge, 1899), pp. 348-51.

[13] Cf. 556/16-557/1, 104/9-15, 511/12-18.

[14] M. R. James, *A Descriptive Catalogue of the Manuscripts Other Than Oriental in the Library of King's College, Cambridge* (Cambridge, 1895), pp. 33-35.

[15] See Dom Aelred Watkin, "Some Manuscripts in the Downside Abbey Library," *The Downside Review*, 59 (1941), 75-92.

of Love, Pore Caitiff, etc., No. 26542, is a series of ascetical tracts; mostly in English. It was written about 1430, and originally belonged to the Dominican nuns of Dartford in Kent. Ff. 168ᵛ-172ʳ include seven meditations in Latin on the Passion, the last two of which are a selection from Suso's *Horologium Sapiencie* and (ff. 171ᵛ-172ʳ) a passage from the *Liber* wherein Christ teaches Mechtild six ways to come to the devotion of tears.[16] The important point here is that both extracts correspond exactly with part of the *Speculum Spiritualium,*[17] a collection ascribed to a Carthusian of Sheen early in the fifteenth century.

(8) *Lincoln, Cathedral Chapter Library, MS 210* is a compilation of 50 prayers and tracts.[18] Richard Rolle and SS. Anselm, Augustine, and Bernard are represented. An exposition of the Lord's Prayer in Latin (ff. 54ᵛ-55ʳ)[19] ends with an explicit reference to *Liber Spiritualis Gracie.*

(9) *Manchester, John Rylands Library, MS 395,* listed as *Miscellanea* and dated after 1480,[20] has selections in Latin and English. F. 90 has excerpts from Rolle, St. Catherine of Siena, St. Birgitta, and two passages in Latin from Mechtild's revelations. The first recounts the things pleasing to our Lord in religious men; the second describes the vision wherein the orders of heavenly hosts catalogue Mechtild's spiritual shortcomings.[21]

(10) *Dublin, Trinity College, MS 277* is a collection of 29 Latin fragments.[22] The sources include the works of Rolle and SS. Anselm, Bernard, Birgitta, and Bonaventure. Two selections from the revelations appear on f. 16ʳ, the first recommending frequent reception of Holy Communion and the second quoting Christ's promise to the soul who has heard Masses devoutly in honour of the saints.[23]

(11) *Durham, University Library, MS Cosin V.III.16,* called *Tractatus Septem,*[24] has devotional matter mostly in Latin. The last entry begins with

[16] Cf. 164/10-165/22.

[17] These pieces are on ff. 131-2 in the printed edition (Paris, 1510). The Downside extracts are of course taken from a manuscript copy.

[18] Reginald Maxwell Woolley, *Catalogue of the Manuscripts of Lincoln Cathedral Chapter Library* (London, 1927), pp. 149-50.

[19] Cf. 575/20-581/20.

[20] A. I. Doyle, "The Work of a Late Fifteenth-Century English Scribe, William Ebesham," *Bulletin of The John Rylands Library* 39 (1956-57), 319; Moses Tyson, "Hand-List of Additions to the Collection of Latin Manuscripts in the John Rylands Library, 1908-1928," *Bulletin of The John Rylands Library* 12 (1928), 604.

[21] The *Booke*'s versions are 251/3-8 and 168/22-170/22 respectively.

[22] T. K. Abbott, *Catalogue of the Manuscripts in the Library of Trinity College, Dublin* (Dublin, 1900), p. 41.

[23] Cf. 466/2-17, 453/7-12.

[24] *Catalogi Veteres Librorum Ecclesiae Cathedralis Dunelm* (Surtees Society, 1838), pp. 168-9.

five fragments (ff. 175ᵛ-177ʳ) from the *Liber*.²⁵ The source is cited, then: "De visione archangeli Gabrielis." The work can be dated after 1489 since it copies a printed book of that year, and it almost certainly came from the brothers' convent of Syon Abbey.²⁶

DEVOTIONAL WORKS

(12) *Speculum Devotorum*,²⁷ a meditation in English on the life of Christ, was written for a woman recipient by a Carthusian, possibly a monk of Sheen. The treatise uses among other sources the *Revelations of St. Birgitta* and the *Orcherd of Syon*, both well known to the Brigittine community of Syon, and alludes to a specific vision wherein Mechtild saw so many angels gathered about the sepulchre of our Lord that they appeared as a wall reaching from the earth to the sky.²⁸

(13) *The Myroure of oure Ladye*²⁹ is in English written for the nuns at Syon as a guide to the liturgy. Date and authorship are not settled issues. The revelations of St. "Maute (Maude)" are referred to twice, once to assure readers that for a good reason it is permissible to miss confession before Mass or divine service, and later to recommend the prayers that Christ taught Mechtild.³⁰

(14) *London, Lambeth Palace, MS 436*,³¹ a copy of Suso's *Horologium Diuinae Sapientiae*, is identified as a gift from John Blacman to the Carthusian monastery at Witham. On one of the folios marked 10 a marginal notation in Latin refers to specific chapters in Suso's work, in the revelations of St. Catherine, and in Mechtild's *Liber*. The section cited from the latter (Part v, ch. 10) contains the exposition of the Pater Noster.

OTHER RECORDS

(15) A list of books donated by the same John Blacman to Witham Charterhouse in mid-century included works by Rolle, SS. Birgitta, Catherine

---

²⁵ Cf. 80/6-82/1, 93/12-95/9, 104/9-20, 492/7-493/7, 510/16-512/2.

²⁶ Information supplied by A. I. Doyle, University of Durham.

²⁷ Rev. John Banks, s.ᴊ., has edited the *Speculum Devotorum* in an unpublished dissertation (Fordham University, 1959).

²⁸ Ibid., p. 248/10-14. The image of angels as a wall appears a few times in the *Booke*; see Note for 181/3-5.

²⁹ Ed. John Henry Blunt (EETS 19, 1873).

³⁰ Ibid., pp. 38-39, 276-7. The passages are taken from parts of two successive chapters in the *Booke*: 473/10-475/19.

³¹ M. R. James and C. Jenkins, *A Descriptive Catalogue of the Manuscripts in the Library of Lambeth Palace* (Cambridge, 1930-32), Part 4, pp. 607-608.

of Siena, and Elizabeth of Schonau. Among these treatises is: "Sancte Matildis vocatur gracia celestis" [32] whose second folio beginning "me diligunt" does not match extant Latin manuscripts.

(16) Some time before 1534, John Whetham, the Carthusian who copied manuscript C, was sent from the London house to the order's monastery Locus Dei at Hinton with some books to be returned when the London prior sent for them. The list of books involved includes *Revelaciones Sancte Matildis.*[33]

(17) The surviving catalogue of Syon Monastery library[34] lists three early sixteenth-century printed copies (M47, M107, M121) and four in manuscript form. Of the latter group three are probably references to Latin texts in whole (M59) and in part (M22, M94); the English version is described: "Reuelaciones beate Matildis in anglico" (M98). The beginnings of the second folios of M59 and M98 do not correspond to extant Latin and English manuscripts.

(18) A document describing the orders and rules of the household of Cicely, duchess of York, indicates that Mechtild's work was read outside the cloister.[35] The pious noblewoman spent much of her time in devout practices; even at mealtime she heard readings from the works of Hilton, SS. Birgitta, Bonaventure, Catherine of Siena, or Mechtild.[36]

(19) The same Cicely in 1495 left her principal literary bequests to her granddaughters Brigitte, a nun of Dartford, and Anne, prioress of Syon.[37] To Brigitte she left the life of St. Catherine of Siena, "a boke of Saint Matilde," and the *Legenda Aurea.*

(20) Earlier, in 1438, Alianora Roos of York left to Dame Joan Courtenay a work called the *Maulde buke.*[38]

(21) In 1491, Thomas Symson left to W. Cok: "j librum de Revelatione Beate Matilde, cum aliis tractatibus in eodem." [39] Both persons were secular priests of York.

---

[32] E. Margaret Thompson, *The Carthusian Order in England,* p. 321.

[33] Ibid., p. 329.

[34] *Catalogue of the Library of Syon Monastery Isleworth,* ed. Mary Bateson.

[35] *A Collection of Ordinances and Regulations for the Government of the Royal Household* (London, 1790), pp. 35-39.

[36] Ibid., p. 37.

[37] *Wills from Doctors' Commons,* edd. J. G. Nichols and J. Bruce (Camden Society, 83, 1863), pp. 2-3.

[38] *Testamenta Eboracensia* 2 (Surtees Society, 30, 1855), p. 66. Alianora Roos was buried in the conventual church of the Carthusian monastery at Mount Grace.

[39] *Testamenta Eboracensia* 3 (Surtees Society, 45, 1865), p. 160.

CONCLUSION

Complete texts of the five-part revelations survive in three Latin and two English manuscripts examined earlier in this study. The evidence set forth in items 15, 16, and 17 above shows that the work existed in at least three additional Latin copies and in one more English version, making a total of nine manuscripts localized in England. The sum is twelve if the lost Latin source (X), the autograph translation (Y), and the parent ancestor (Z) of the extant English copies are not among the untraced manuscripts. Copies mentioned in the three wills might bring the number to fifteen.

B. THE *BOOKE* IN THE ENGLISH MYSTICAL TRADITION

Investigation has disclosed no definite facts concerning the migration of the *Liber* from Germany and its translation into English. Its early history in England, though shrouded in obscurity, was probably shared by that large body of other Continental writings, especially those from the German and Flemish mystics, that circulated in Latin and eventually in English during the fifteenth century. It is beyond question that books by and about St. Elizabeth of Schonau, Mechtild, Tauler, Suso, and Ruysbroek appeared in libraries side by side with native treatises and the traditional store of religious classics. What is uncertain is the identity of the agents who diffused the material from abroad in England. David Knowles acknowledged that the mainstream of English mysticism is indebted in part to the foreign tradition;[40] Miss Hope Emily Allen, conceding the same point, speculated that pious works of German and Flemish origin might have circulated both in literary and oral form as a result of the thriving wool trade between the English merchant cities and the Low Countries, and possibly too because of the presence of German and Flemish aliens in such places as Lynn and London.[41] More reliable evidence points to the religious orders, notably the Carthusians, as the carriers of Latin manuscripts into England. Records indicate that the English monks had active relations with their brethren abroad, that Flemish monks were transferred to the new foundation at Sheen in 1414, that books were exchanged within the English province and between it and the foreign Charterhouses, that Carthusians were active in importing and translating Latin copies of Continental religious tracts, and that the brethren at Sheen

---

[40] *The Religious Orders in England*, 3 vols. (Cambridge, 1950-59), 2: 121-2.
[41] S. B. Meech and Hope Emily Allen, edd., *The Book of Margery Kempe* (EETS 212, 1940), pp. liii-liv.

were translators, scribes, and donors of books at nearby Syon.[42] Documentation already noted links Latin and English versions of Mechtild's revelations to Syon and to a Carthusian environment.[43] The assumption then that the *Liber* was introduced into England by the Carthusians soon after the foundation of Sheen and translated by a monk there or by a brother at Syon is not unreasonable.[44] But the facts support this only as a possibility.

The *Booke* itself offers scant information about the circumstances of the translation. In his prologue and epilogue the English author is vague about himself although he says nothing that contradicts the natural assumption that he was a religious laboring for a group of other religious who could not read Latin. But the makeup of his audience is uncertain because of conflicting references to his readers and listeners: in E they are addressed as sisters twice and brothers and sisters three times, whereas in B they are referred to as brothers and sisters throughout (see Note for 65/13). This confusion, undoubtedly the result of at least two layers of transcription, prevents us from determining with confidence whether the *Booke* was written initially for the Syon community. Syon was a double convent although of course not the only one at the time. On the other hand, the brethren there could read Latin, and we must remember that later scribes often adapted their copies for specific audiences. The conclusion is that there is no decisive proof of Brigittine or Carthusian provenance, but the evidence does support the claim that the dissemination of Mechtild's account in fifteenth-century England is in large measure due to Carthusian auspices.

The earliest specific date associated with the work in England is 1438 when Alianora Roos of York made a bequest of her *Maulde buke*. The surmise that this was in English is compatible with the conclusions obtained from the textual examinations of B and E indicating that they were most likely copied during the second and third quarters of the century. Thus it appears quite certain that the autograph translation was undertaken before mid-century, possibly before 1438.[45]

---

[42] On these points see Bateson, *Catalogue of the Library of Syon Monastery*, p. xii; E. Colledge, ed., *The Mediaeval Mystics of England* (New York, 1961), p. 83; Doyle, "A Text Attributed to Ruusbroec Circulating in England," pp. 157, 161; Thompson, *The Carthusian Order in England*, pp. 267, 287, 299, 313-32. Nicholas Love, prior of Mount Grace, translated the *Mirror of the Life of Christ* from Latin about 1400; earlier an unknown Carthusian translated the *Mirror of Simple Souls* from French.

[43] It is noteworthy that the language and possible ownership of manuscript E and the bequests in three wills attest to the currency of the revelations in the north of England. The Carthusians had three houses in the northern counties.

[44] N. F. Blake, "Revelations of St. Matilda," *Notes and Queries* 218 (1973), 323-5.

[45] Miss Allen believed that the *Liber* was known in English before Margery Kempe had her own experiences recorded in 1436-8. (*The Book of Margery Kempe*, p. lxvi.)

Testimony has shown that the revelations enjoyed a respectable readership among religious and literate lay people and was considered worthy of such company as Hilton, Rolle, SS. Birgitta, Catherine of Siena, and Elizabeth of Schonau in libraries and in compilations of mystical writings. The modern reader might find it difficult to account for the popularity of the *Booke*, a work which is an adequate translation at best but unoriginal in its approach and elementary in its spirituality. In the fifteenth century, however, the treatise was sure to command a large and enthusiastic reading because it was a recent and comparatively unknown text and because it described ecstatic experiences in the form of a spiritual biography.[46] Then too its eminently "practical" character must have appealed to the simple religious for whom it was intended. Speculative mysticism such as analyzed and fostered in the *Cloud of Unknowing* was not the piety of the masses; that tract and kindred pieces must have been of limited value in the average convent, and spiritual directors were surely careful to reserve the intellectual strong meat of theoretical mystical literature for those adept in the subtleties of the highest stages of contemplation. The ascetical nature of the revelations with its multitudinous exempla, prayers, and devotions was far more satisfactory to a wide range of unlearned readers.[47] On the grounds of homely piety and ardent devotion, the *Booke* conformed in part to a type of medieval English spirituality that went back to the *Ancrene Riwle*. Mechtild's account has none of the practical experience and wise counsel that distinguishes the *Riwle* among religious manuals, but both treatises have an absence of technique and system and are only incidentally concerned with the attainment of pure contemplation.[48] The *Booke* also harmonized with the temperament that was drawn to the personal fervour and the non-speculative Christocentric treatments in writings by Rolle and Hilton. Other features, such as Rolle's quality of passionate subjectivism and Hilton's attempts to analyze the contemplative states and to modify certain ambiguous ideas and expressions, are not found in Mechtild's revelations.

[46] Before St. Birgitta's death in 1373 Latin copies of her revelations were available in England where they aroused great interest. See William Patterson Cumming, ed., *The Revelations of Saint Birgitta* (EETS 178, 1929), p. xxix. Miss Allen prints the sources attesting to the vogue of St. Hildegarde, St. Elizabeth, and Suso in England: *The Book of Margery Kempe*, pp. liii-liv.

[47] The status of the revelations as a treatise of practical mysticism is shown by the excerpts and references in contemporary anthologies. Most passages present pious exercises or recommendations for improving moral conduct; only three refer to the imaginative descriptions of the visions.

[48] Nevertheless mystical union is understood to be the ultimate and inevitable culmination of all the efforts to achieve perfection in this life. See Introduction by Dom Gerard Sitwell, O.S.B., to M. B. Salu's modern translation of *The Ancrene Riwle* (London, 1955).

The contemporary standing of the *Booke* was undoubtedly influenced by the estimate of church authorities, and that estimate in turn was formed by the *Booke*'s handling of four delicate subjects in a manner that allayed official censure. These subjects, always of import in assessing mystical literature but of vital concern in fifteenth-century England, were identified by Eric Colledge in his Introduction to *The Chastising of God's Children*: "(a) the recognition and combat of heresy, (b) the repression of 'enthusiasm', (c) the 'discerning of spirits' and (d) the claims of the liturgy against private devotions." [49] None of these topics is discussed overtly in the *Booke*, but the implicit view on each supports orthodox opinion.

The most obvious sign of religious conflict at the time was the Wycliffite movement, which signified its dissent principally by attacking the religious orders and the hierarchy.[50] In terms of this discord the *Booke*, while not in any sense directing its remarks to critics, becomes a staunch ally of the traditional institutions. Profuse commendations are heaped on the religious life; virgins are extolled; St. Benedict and by extension the monastic life are called supporting pillars of the Church; the prayers and meditations of contemplatives are declared to be of immeasurable benefit to fellow Christians; and disrespect and disobedience to the clergy, especially those in authority, are regarded as grave offenses. Heresies of foreign origin had not penetrated into English religious life to any appreciable extent, but watchful ecclesiastics were on the alert to detect any taint of doctrinal error or dangerous interpretation.[51] The *Booke* lends no support whatsoever to extremist views of the non-conformist German and Flemish sects, such as the beghards' claim to identification with God in mystical union or the Brethren of the Free Spirit's insistence on substituting a dissolute "liberty of spirit" for church authority and moral discipline. On the contrary, there is an emphatic rejection of the pantheistic doctrine of absorption in God: in a re-creation of the Nativity, Mechtild sees the Virgin Mary kiss her child "þorowe whiche kusse sche was oonyde fullye to the blessede trinite as moche as euere hitt was possible anye manne or womane to be onyde to God withowtyne personale oonyoun" (94/7-10); elsewhere Christ promises communion with the soul, but not union of essences: "I schalle multyplye my gyftes in þee inasmoche as itt es possibille any man to haffe" (357/14-15). Like most mystical treatises

[49] Ed. with Joyce Bazire (Oxford, 1957), p. 47. The present writer's ensuing discussion of these points is heavily indebted to Father Colledge's analysis of the prevailing religious climate.

[50] Knowles, *The Religious Orders in England*, 2: 98-106, summarizes these charges.

[51] See Allen, *The Book of Margery Kempe*, p. 311, note 116/12, for evidence showing apprehension on the part of English authorities in regard to Continental heresies.

the *Booke* is open to the usual perils of misinterpretation if the hyperbolic and metaphorical language is taken literally.[52] Actually, slight attention is given to the matter of deification, and even then the expression is usually in the common similitudes of spiritual devotion: "I am in the ande þowe erte in me as fysche in the watere" (376/7-8). The stress throughout is on positive endeavors. Praise of mortifications and active prayer is far removed from the assertions of false "natural" rest made by the Quietists. The spiritual rest-fulness recommended in the revelations is the trustful soul's ease in the midst of adversities or the true contemplative's repose in God. On these themes that were associated with incipient heresies the *Booke* could be endorsed as blameless and so it avoided the hostile criticism that rendered some foreign writings suspect.

It also avoided the official strictures levelled at "enthusiasm." Authorities were inclined to discourage and deplore any hint of spiritual extravagance or singularity and to be vehement in opposing the habits and beliefs of those whose mysticism was closely identified with physical phenomena. "Enthu-siasts" such as Margery Kempe with her loud cries and Richard Rolle with his emotional rhapsodies of "canor, calor, and dulcor" were frequently reproved openly or by inferences,[53] not so much because of any alleged heresies, but because their abnormal behavior and extraordinary claims of divine favors were considered indiscreet and potentially dangerous. The moral disintegra-tion feared by churchmen was already a grave reality on the Continent where enthusiasm had perpetrated a string of perverse cults. Devotees, it was felt, were particularly susceptible to egoism and pride and the despairing aridity left in the soul in the wake of sensory transports. Another fear was that the unwary enthusiast is more easily victimized by the devil who is notoriously clever in disguising diabolic possession as spiritual graces. This danger makes the discernment of spirits an immensely important factor in judging the validity and usefulness of a mystical treatise. Any tract with a "marvelous" character and purporting to relate personal revelations was subjected to close scrutiny for signs of hypocrisy, illusion, and wicked influences.[54] It is very

[52] See Clark, *The Great German Mystics*, pp. 17, 47, 61, for the misuse of Eckhart's doctrines by ignorant and superficial heretics. The beghards were said to have quoted Eckhart in their defense.

[53] See Allen, *The Book of Margery Kempe*, pp. lvii-lviii; *Writings Ascribed to Richard Rolle, Hermit of Hampole, and Materials for his Biography* (London, 1927), pp. 335, 529-37; Walter Hilton, *The Scale of Perfection*, ed. Dom Gerard Sitwell, o.s.b. (London, 1953), Book 1, chs. 10, 12, 26, 47; "Of the Song of Angels," in *The Cell of Self-Knowledge*, ed. Edmund G. Gardner (London, 1925), pp. 68-70; *The Cloud of Unknowing and The Book of Privy Counselling*, ed. Phyliis Hodgson (EETS 218, 1944), pp. 90-91.

[54] See "A Pistle of Discrecioun of Stirings" and "A Tretis of Discrescyon of Spirites," in *Deonise Hid Diuinite*, ed. Phyllis Hodgson (EETS 231, 1955), pp. 62 et seq.

nearly remarkable that the *Booke* qualifies in the tests for the suppression of enthusiasm and the discernment of spirits since it is the record of a visionary's ecstatic experiences and physical phenomena are plentiful. Mechtild's personal conduct, however, is consistently edifying and bears no resemblance to the enthusiast's vainglory and independence. She is aware of the devil's machinations in sending false visions and is properly disinclined to accept any at face value; she displays a holy dread in the course of her communion with God; she makes studious efforts to avoid ostentatious behavior; and she is modestly reluctant to allow the revelations to become public knowledge. Her piety is almost wholly interior; rarely is there mention of unusual external actions. Furthermore, the interpretation of divine favors fits the most exacting standards of orthodoxy. The familiar relations between Christ and Mechtild's soul are depicted as rewards for her assiduous cultivation of the Rule and the counsels of perfection. The splendours and curiosities of her visions are always linked with explicit recommendations for the increase of prayerful fervour. Even the descriptions of the periods of tormenting temptations and spiritual dryness are not occasions of despair but of exemplary confidence and submission. The severest adversary of enthusiasm and its concomitant ills would admit that the *Booke*'s visions and locutions operate not as ends and delights in themselves but as stimuli for the increase of piety.

On the issue of the proper place and value of private devotions the *Booke* conforms to the official position that the Hours were to be recited in Latin as canonically required and that vernacular prayers were to be relegated to other times. In Mechtild's convent in Helfta, where there was apparently no problem about the use and intelligibility of Latin among the cultivated nuns, the divine Office and the conventual Mass formed the core of the daily liturgical exercises. Even so, as the *Liber* bears witness, there were opportunity and sanction for the recitation of Paters, Aves, and other "inspired" prayers. But the audience of English religious who could not read the *Liber* might have belonged to an order that was enjoined to recite the Office in Latin whether it was understood or not, or perhaps they were a congregation some members of which were permitted to substitute vernacular prayers provided they did not disturb other members of the choir. Whatever the case, the point is that the *Booke* emphasizes the primary obligation to execute the service faithfully and fervently: concrete exhortations are made for zeal in performing the duty of the Office,[55] frequent admonitions are directed to the sluggish and inattentive, and specific penances are listed for faults of

---

[55] The paraphrases from the revelations that appear in *The Myroure of oure Ladye* (see above, p. 50, item 13) include an earnest plea to view the service as a "paynge of dette."

neglect or distraction. The *Booke* provided an exemplar for the primacy of prescribed worship over private exercises even as it served as a compendium for extra-liturgical devotions.

Aside from its inoffensive management of these sensitive topics, the revelations had positive appeal in feeding current tastes for certain devotions. The cult of the Sacred Heart in England, like its counterpart on the Continent, had its roots in the early history of the Church, but had reached a recognizable stage of development by the end of the fourteenth century when images of representations of the Heart appeared not only in manuscripts but also in carvings of wood and stone, in metal work and paintings, on banners and standards, and in stained glass windows.[56] The earliest references in English religious literature have been traced to the *Ancrene Riwle*,[57] but they grow more frequent in the fourteenth and fifteenth centuries when they are seen in *Piers Plowman, The Pearl*, in one of the anthologies of Rolle and his imitators, and in the tenth "showing" of Julian of Norwich.[58] Clearly this devotion described with loving affection and veneration was responsible for no small part of the *Booke*'s popularity in medieval England. The same is true of the even more widespread devotion to the agonies and crucifixion of Christ. Rolle, to name only one native mystic, was an ardent disciple of the Passion, but he represents a development of a treatment centuries old.[59] Mechtild's revelations on this material fell in line with a practice well established in English spiritual life. Moreover, since the tenderness so typical of her piety as a whole dominates the imagery and sentiment of these visions, the *Booke* avoided the more repellent and gross evocations of the physical sufferings of Christ.[60]

The importance and influence of the *Booke* in the English mystical tradition are assured of some status because it belonged to the class of newly available writings of Continental women mystics. As such it might have contributed to the foundation of a vogue for female mysticism. Sr. Anna Maria Reynolds, in her study of the influences on Dame Julian, suggested that the

[56] Gilbert Dolan, o.s.b., "Devotion to the Sacred Heart in Medieval England," *Dublin Review*, 120 (1897), 373-85. Devotion to the Five Wounds, Precious Blood, and Sacred Heart is discussed in Douglas Gray, *Themes and Images in the Medieval English Religious Lyric* (London, 1972), pp. 132-5. See also above, p. 43.

[57] By implication, however, they are found in Bede, and are not original to him. See Colledge, ed., *The Mediaeval Mystics of England*, pp. 10-11.

[58] Margaret Anne Williams, *Glee-Wood* (New York, 1949), pp. 464-7.

[59] See *English Writings of Richard Rolle, Hermit of Hampole*, ed. Hope Emily Allen (Oxford, 1931), pp. 17-36 and notes.

[60] Like Suso's *Little Book of Eternal Wisdom*, trans. James M. Clark (New York, 1953), pp. 14-15, the *Booke* concentrates on the Passion to demonstrate how man can share in the redemptive work of Christ.

chief importance in England of the writings of SS. Mechtild, Catherine of Siena, and Birgitta was that they helped to weaken the contemporary native prejudice against women aspiring to mystical experiences.[61] From the point of view of method and content, Julian's work owes nothing to her predecessors overseas,[62] but the case might be different with another celebrated woman's spiritual autobiography, Margery Kempe's *Book*. Although Margery's title as mystic has been challenged, she was nevertheless a writer of pious feeling and considerable experience. Her remarkably outspoken work reveals much on contemporary religious trends and attitudes. She knew of the native English mystics: a friendly priest read to her from Rolle and Hilton, and she herself visited Julian at Norwich. The only book of foreign origin she mentions is the *Revelations of Saint Birgitta*, but this does not necessarily rule out a familiarity with others. Miss Allen has commented on the circumstances that made Margery possibly open to foreign influences: her residence in Lynn, an important station on the trade and pilgrim routes; a Dominican confessor who might have introduced her, via oral channels, to the writings of the German nun-mystics; her son's stay in Germany and Margery's trip thither with her daughter-in-law; and her travels overseas in company with those among whom popular hagiographical accounts must have circulated. All this of course does not prove that Margery was consciously influenced by, or even knew in any direct way, the revelations of Mechtild. It does suggest that she had the opportunity to absorb reminiscences of the foreign women mystics among whom Mechtild figures.[63] The welcome accorded to these accounts set a precedent which did much to credit Margery in the judgment of ecclesiastical authorities who otherwise would have found elements of her spirituality objectionable.[64] This seems to be the only explanation for the extent and quality of the clerical support that Margery did enjoy and for her own conviction that an autobiographical record surveying portions of her own life and replete with visions and revelations was necessary and useful.

The *Booke*'s distinction as part of this contemporary trend and its worth as an edifying demonstration of ascetic piety fairly well define its significance in the English mystical tradition.

---

[61] "Some Literary Influences in the Revelations of Julian of Norwich," *Leeds Studies in English and Kindred Languages*, 7 (1952), 18-28.

[62] Julian's writing has none of the prophetical and polemical elements found in St. Catherine's and St. Birgitta's, and there is no similarity between Julian's intensive reflections on the doctrinal implications of her visions and Mechtild's flowing descriptions of her ecstatic raptures.

[63] Miss Allen has remarked on some similarities with these mystics in notes to *The Book of Margery Kempe*, pp. 255-350.

[64] Ibid., p. lv.

4

Principles of Editing

Manuscript E has many faulty readings, some attributable to a corrupt Latin source, others derived from the translator's mistakes and misunderstandings, and still others caused by past and present scribal errors. But it must be remembered that the autograph translation was not consistently faithful to the *Liber*, ranging as it did from close rendering to free paraphrase and often including gratuitous commentary. It would therefore be hazardous to emend E's many ambiguous passages by bringing them into conformity with the literal meaning of C. Such a procedure would involve wholesale and arbitrary editorial interference and would alter the Middle English text on a significant scale. In order to avoid the danger of distorting the *Booke*, it was decided to list in the Notes to the text the Latin readings of the incorrect and confusing Middle English passages. Conjectures concerning probable original Middle English readings are also listed in the Notes. This edition replaces readings common to both E and B in places (e.g., 108/3, 199/7, 459/15, 16, 460/11) where a single word restores the sense of the Latin. Otherwise E's text is emended only (1) when B's variant is clearly superior, either because it corresponds to the Latin or because it has the claim to better sense, or (2) when a change is justified by a comparison with a duplicate passage elsewhere in E (e.g., the errors in the Table of Chapters are corrected by reference to the headings of the chapters, and vice versa).

The spelling of emendations adapted from B has been altered to make them conform with the usual spelling in E. All changes to the basic text are enclosed in square brackets, and manuscript readings appear in the apparatus. One exception to this practice concerns the numbers of chapters in the Table of Chapters and in the chapter headings. In the manuscript these are occasionally omitted or misnumbered; *capitulum* sporadically precedes the numbers; digits are sometimes arabic, sometimes roman, sometimes both. In this edition the numbering is regularized throughout without comment, except that the apparatus records incorrect combinations of arabic and roman digits (e.g., 293/16), the first misnumbering in each part in the *Booke* (e.g., 8/18), and any later correction of the numbering within the part (e.g., 310/7).

Contractions have been expanded in accordance with the common spellings of the same or similar words when written in full. The various strokes and signs used significantly and with regularity, as noted in the description of the manuscript earlier in this Introduction, allow for expansions about which there are no doubts. But because of irregularity in practice, the function of the macron in final syllables is uncertain. In this edition the macron in the syllable *-ion* is taken to mean a missing *i* or *n*; in other word endings the macron is expanded to a final *-e* or *-n*, never *ne*. The symbol over *u-n* combinations is interpreted as an intervening *-au-* when those letters are called for; otherwise it is ignored. In the name John there is some uncertainty about the meaning of the stroked *h* in the manuscript's usual spelling "Iohn," and in the rare "Iohis" (3/16) and "Ihone" (105/8). The name has been expanded here to "Ioh*a*n." In the manuscript, abbreviations in Greek for Jesus are usual; throughout this edition the spelling "Ihesu" appears without italics. Greek letters used for the full name "Jesus Christ" in Latin passages have been silently expanded to Latin forms in 129/9, 304/9, 514/14. The forms & and *et c.* represent the symbols used in the manuscript. When *ff* appears at the beginning of a word it is reproduced as *f* or *F*.

Latin phrases are italicized. Paragraphing and modern punctuation have been introduced. Capitals have been affixed to proper names, feasts of the liturgy, words at the beginning of sentences, and only "God" and "Ihesu Criste" among the various terms that designate the deity ("fadere," "sonne," "holye goste," "trinite," "lorde," etc.). Certain word groups, often written separately in E ("alle be itte," "in als moche"), have been silently joined to conform to modern usage. A hyphen joins words intended as a unit ("here warde," "for spetede").

The apparatus states rejected readings in E as well as the manuscript's alterations and marginalia. Standard abbreviations *add.* (added), *can.* (cancelled), *corr.* (corrected), *ins.* (inserted), *mar.* (margin), *trs.* (transposed) are employed for the usual purposes. E^c indicates that the rubrics are in a hand other than that of the scribe of E. The apparatus also records all substantive variants in B. Certain differences (e.g., fro] from; before] tofore) recur with great frequency and would make the apparatus uselessly lengthy if quoted throughout; these are recorded several times but are not noted after the signal "*and elsewhere*" has been given in the apparatus. Mere spelling and dialect differences are customarily ignored, but some linguistically interesting variants are pointed out in the first ten folios and are followed by the notation "*and elsewhere*." In stating the variants of a word, the hyphen represents a detachable part of that word whose difference is of no importance (e.g., peynfulle] -fullye). A superscript number added to the lemma indicates that the variant refers to the designated instance of that word in the line of the text (e.g., of²] *om.* B). A superscript number added to a letter in the variant refers to the designated instance of that letter in the word (e.g., sawe] seye, e¹ *ins.* B). Marginalia in B have not been recorded unless they are alterations to the text.

The Booke of Gostlye Grace

SCHEMATIC GUIDE TO THE FICHE

FICHE 1: Table of contents — Book 1. c. 10

[Title page]	1 Capitula prime partis				
14					
28					
42					
56	57 Capitula quinte partis				
70 [Prima pars] c. 1			74 c. 2		
84	85 c. 5	86 c. 6	88 c. 7		

Pp. 1-97

				25 Capitula secunde partis		
			38 Capitula tercie partis			
49 Capitula quarte partis						
		65 Incipit Liber Sancte Matildie	66 Furste prologe		68 Secundus prologus	
			80 c. 3		82 c. 4	
	92 c. 8	93 c. 9			96 c. 10	

FICHE 2: **Book 1, c. 11 — Book 1, c. 42**

98	99 c. 11	100 c. 12				104 c. 13
112		114 c. 17			117 c. 18	
126 c. 22		128 c. 23				
140		142 c. 26				
154 c. 29		156 c. 30	157 c. 31			160 c. 32
168						174 c. 34
182 c. 38	183 c. 39					188 c. 40

Pp. 98 — 195

			108		110	111
			c. 14		c. 15	c. 16
119		121				125
c. 19		c. 20				c. 21
		135	136			
		c. 24	c. 25			
		149			152	
		c. 27			c. 28	
						167
						c. 33
			178	179	180	
			c. 35	c. 36	c. 37	
		191			194	
		c. 41			c. 42	

FICHE 3: Book 1, c. 43 — Book 1, c. 77

196			200		202
c. 43			c. 44		c. 45
210	211		214	215	
c. 46	c. 47		c. 48	c. 49	
224				229	
c. 53				c. 54	
238		240			
		c. 58			
252		255			
		c. 62			
266		269		271	272
		c. 66		c. 67	c. 68
280		282	284		286
		c. 71	c. 72		c. 73

Pp. 196 — 293

217 c. 50	218 c. 51			221 c. 52		
		233 c. 55		235 c. 56		237 c. 57
245 c. 59				249 c. 60		251 c. 61
259 c. 63				263 c. 64		265 c. 65
		275 c. 69				279 c. 70
	288 c. 74	289 c. 75 c. 76				293 c. 77

FICHE 4: Book 1, c. 78 — Book 2, c. 35

294				298 c. 78		
308 c. 81		310 c. 82		312 c. 83		314 c. 84
322	323 c. 87		325 Secunda pars c. 1			328 c. 2
336 c. 5 c. 6	337 c. 7	338 c. 8	339 c. 9	340 c. 10	341 c. 11	342 c. 12
350 c. 17	351 c. 18		353 c. 19			
364 c. 22		366 c. 23			369 c. 24	
378	379 c. 28			382 c. 29	383 c. 30	

Pp.294 — 391

	302				306	
	c. 79				c. 80	
315					320	
c. 85					c. 86	
						335
						c. 3 c. 4
343	344		346	347		
c. 13	c. 14		c. 15	c. 16		
357						363
c. 20						c. 21
		373			376	377
		c. 25			c. 26	c. 27
385	386	387		389	390	
c. 31	c. 32	c. 33		c. 34	c. 35	

FICHE 5: Book 2, c. 36 — Book 3, c. 39

392		394		397	398
		c. 36		c. 37	c. 38
406		408			412
c. 42		Tercia pars c. 1			c. 2
420	421				426
	c. 5				c. 6
434		436	437		440
c. 10		c. 11	c. 12		c. 13
448			451	453	454
			c. 17	c. 18	c. 19
462	463		465	466	
	c. 25		c. 26	c. 27	
476			479	481	482
c. 33			c. 34	c. 35	c. 36

Pp. 392 — 489

		401		403	404	
		c. 39		c. 40	c. 41	
	414			417		
	c. 3			c. 4		
	428		430		432	
	c. 7		c. 8		c. 9	
441			444			447
c. 14			c. 15			c. 16
455		457		459	460	461
c. 20		c. 21		c. 22	c. 23	c. 24
469		471		473	474	475
c. 28		c. 29		c. 30	c. 31	c. 32
	484		486	487		
	c. 37		c. 38	c. 39		

FICHE 6: Book 3, c. 40 — Book 5, c. 14

490 c. 40 c. 41		492 c. 42	493 c. 43		496 Quarta pars c. 1
504 c. 7			507 c. 8	509 c. 9	510 c. 10
518	519 c. 15	520 c. 16		523 c. 17	
532	533 c. 24 c. 25	534 c. 26 c. 27	535 c. 28 c. 29	536 c. 30 c. 31	537 c. 32
546			549 c. 36	551 c. 37	552 c. 38
560			563 c. 5	565 c. 6	
574	575 c. 10				580 c. 11

	498	499	500	501	502	
	c. 2	c. 3	c. 4	c. 5	c. 6	
	512		514	515		517
	c. 11		c. 12	c. 13		c..14
	526	527	528	529	530	531
	c. 18	c. 19	c. 20	c. 21	c. 22	c. 23
	540		542			545
	c. 33		c. 34			c. 35
		555			558	559
		V pars c. 1 c. 2			c. 3	c. 4
	568	569	570			
	c. 7	c. 8	c. 9			
581		583		585		
c. 12		c. 13		c. 14		

FICHE 7: Book 5, c. 15 — Explicit

588	589			591		593	
c. 15	c. 16			c. 17		c. 18	
602							

Pp. 588 — 613

		596	597	598	599		
		c. 19	c. 20	c. 21	c. 22		
					613 Explicit		

Notes to the Text

(All scriptural quotations are cited
from the Vulgate edition of the Bible.)

1/3. *Booke of Gostlye Grace*: This translation of *Liber Spiritualis Gracie* is repeated on 70/4, but the alternative English form—*The Booke of Spyrytualle Grace*—is more common: 37/20, 65/14, 407/7, etc. The "special grace" from the earliest Latin title is referred to: 71/8-9, 365/17-18, 585/20-21.

26/4. *and whate alle this betokenede*: A full sentence should properly follow this; it is included in the rubric (328/16-19). Its omission here might be another example of homoeoteleuton in the ancestor of E and B.

45/15. *penalte*: suffering. According to the OED, this spelling is not found before 1500. Cf. the earlier form "penalite" 469/7.

60/16-17. *Ande howe ... prayere*: The sentence is misplaced, being a re-statement of the "v benefettys" referred to in the next entry 60/21. The matter is treated in ch. 11 (581/8-13).

65/7. *Malde*: The other English versions of Mechtild's name are "Molde" 126/8, 138/5, 147/8, etc. and "Moolte" 198/22. B uses "Molte" twice, otherwise "Mawte."

65/13. *sustrene*: Sisters are addressed again 612/13; elsewhere (67/11, 125/4, 439/16) the audience is referred to as brothers and sisters.

65/18. *laste chapitere*: 406/10-407/14.

65/19. *laste partye*: 588/10-15.

66/12. *the endeys of worldeys*: This assertion is repeated at the end of the revelations (611/11-12). Emile Mâle in *The Gothic Image: Religious Art in France of the Thirteenth Century*, trans. Dora Nussey, from 3rd French ed. (New York, 1958), pp. 355-6, reminds us that during the thirteenth century the imminence of the Last Judgment was a familiar thought. Earlier, Joachim of Flora and St. Hildegarde had prophesied that the end of the world would occur near the close of the twelfth century, but later writers fixed 1300 as the date. Vincent of Beauvais concluded his *Speculum Historiale* (c. 1250) with an ominous account of the Last Judgment.

67/6. *sche tolde in partye...*: There are additional references describing the compilation as an incomplete account of Mechtild's visions; cf. 407/7-14, 600/10. The same statement is made in the longer version; see *Revelationes*, 2: 2.

67/20. *Saynte Austyne*: De Doctrina Christiana, 4, 11; *P.L.* 34, col. 100.

68/4-5. *profytabelle ande lernynge*: Scribal error appears to have caused this asymmetric coordination. C: "utilitas et instructio."

69/20. *gladnesse*: This word and "gladdelye" translates forms of "gratitudo" here and 133/9, 292/6, 354/22, 478/9, 498/21, 515/10, 548/12.

69/22. *slewth*: This word translates "tepor" (113/9), "torpor" (450/17), as well as "accidia" (145/3). The failing is more than simple laziness; it is negligence in performing one's duties to God. A comprehensive study is Siegfried Wenzel's *The Sin of Sloth: "Acedia" in Medieval Thought and Literature* (Chapel Hill, 1960).

71/3. *be reuelacion*: This refers to the vision that culminates with the assertion of Mechtild's "election" (171/8-9).

71/15. *howse of nunnys*: The convent at Rodardsdorf.

71/20-21. *sche bade pare*: The custom of receiving young children into monasteries was not uncommon among the Benedictines at this time; see Dom Ursmer Berlière, "Le recrutement dans les monastères bénédictins aux xiiie et xive siècles," *Académie royale de Belgique*, 18, fasc. 6 (1924), 5-14. The Council of Trent decreed that religious profession could not be made before the completion of the sixteenth year; see Rev. H. J. Schroeder, O.P., *Canons and Decrees of the Council of Trent* (St. Louis, 1941), p. 226. Mechtild's sister was elected abbess at the age of nineteen, and St. Gertrude entered the convent school at Helfta before she was six years old.

74/21. *Erit...*: Isai. 11: 5.

75/18-19. *ande with ... askes*: E freely adapts erroneous C. S reads: "in cujus aspectu mellifluo cinis ad nihilum est redactus."

75/21. *Here ... sodaynlye*: This comment does not appear in C.

76/3-4. *here perfeccion and affeccion*: This senseless phrasing follows C. S reads: "omnisque ejus imperfectio Filii Dei perfectione altissima perfecta."

76/20-21. *a pype alle of golde*: C reads: "fistula aurea." The "fistula" was the reed by means of which the precious Blood was received. It was in general use in the Western Church until about the twelfth century at which time Communion under one kind became the usual practice. In some religious houses the use of the "fistula" lingered for a while longer, and its use has never been discontinued in the solemn Papal Mass. "Pugillaris" is another Latin term for the vessel. See Archdale A. King, *Liturgy of the Roman Church* (Milwaukee, 1957), pp. 402-403.

77/4. *Laudem*...: Apoc. 19, 5; Antiphon, 3 Nocturn for the feast of All Saints.

77/21. *Deum*...: Joann. 20: 17.

80/6. *the tyme*: Feast of the Annunciation.

81/12. *Ecce*...: Luc. 1: 38; gospel for the feast of the Annunciation.

82/10-11. *Thowe erte*...: Cf. Joann. 17: 21-23.

83/1-2. *fulle replete ... wyne*: This simile recalls St. Bernard's celebrated image: "ut divino debriatus amore" in *De Diligendo Deo*, 10, *P.L.*, 182, col. 990.

86/21. *offyce*: When used in reference to the Mass, this term usually identifies the first words of the Introit.

87/7, 17. *voyce of myne ioye; ioye of myne voyce*: Both C and S interchange the phrases in the four "maners" but E's wordings do not conform to either Latin version consistently.

87/12. *Remittuntur*...: Luc. 7: 48, 50.

87/17. See Note 87/7.

87/19. *Come*...: Cf. Cantic. 2: 13, 14.

88/2. *Veni*...: Antiphon, Office of Virgins.

88/8. *Venite*...: Matt. 25: 34.

88/15. *tyme of masse*: Third Saturday of Advent; the Introit begins: "Veni et ostendi nobis faciem tuam."

89/1. *a thowsaundefalde sunnys*: The association of bright light with the manifestations of God is used extensively throughout these visions. It is, of course, a commonplace in mystical writings and has its roots in Scripture: "Et orietur vobis timentibus nomen meum sol justitiae, ..." (Malach. 4: 2).

89/18. *veerse*: Psal. 18: 6.

89/19. *He ioyede als a gyaunte*: St. Bernard has an extended simile of Christ as a giant running a course: *In Cantica*, 21, *P.L.*, 183, col. 876. The *Booke* uses the image as an example of zeal and fervent devotion; see 294/20 et seq., 309/1 et seq. The Dominican William Peraldus in *Summa de vitiis et virtutibus* (c. 1236) offers the figure as a model for overcoming the sin of "acedia." See Wenzel, *The Sin of Sloth*, p. 104.

90/10. *Sylke ... þrede*: C reads: "Sericum rubeum cum bonum est forcius est alio."

90/11-16. *rede ... grene ... whyet*: Color symbolism is prevalent throughout these revelations. In most cases, Mechtild associates white with innocence; see 120/11, 280/20. In the medieval liturgy a considerable variety of interpretation was observed; see Dom Louis Gougaud, *Dévotions et pratiques ascétiques du moyen âge* (Maredsous, 1925), pp. 212-14, and King, *Liturgy of the Roman Church*, pp. 115-16.

90/17. *benignite*: C: "benignitatis"; S: "humanitatis."

91/14. *in the prestes stede*: Christ appears again at Communion time in the priest's stead on 270/16-17.

91/16. *a lampe brennynge*: William Durandus, a thirteenth-century churchman, notes that virgins are pictorially represented carrying lamps, a graphic allusion to the parable of the wise and foolish virgins (Matt. 25: 1). See *The Symbolism of Churches and Church Ornaments* (A translation of the first book of the *Rationale Divinorum Officiorum* by Durandus), trans. Rev. John Mason Neale and Rev. Benjamin Webb, 3rd ed. (London, 1906), p. 49.

92/17. *Miserere*: Psal. 150.

95/1. *helde hym betwyx here aarmys*: This action occurs again, 97/15 and 102/12-13. Woolf, *The English Religious Lyric*, p. 145, remarks that several women mystics of Germany and Italy had the privilege of holding the Christ child in their visions. See Note 136/20.

95/18-19. *be infucion of love oonely of Godde*: St. Bernard makes the same point; the soul cannot procure this sweetness of love by its own diligence. See *De Diligendo Deo*, 10, *P.L.*, 182, col. 992: "quippe quod Dei potentiae est dare cui vult, non humanae industriae assequi."

97/6. *Salue...*: St. Ambrose's morning hymn to the Trinity is sung during Monday's Lauds. The word Salue does not precede the modern version. See *The Hymns of the Breviary and Missal*, ed. Rev. Matthew Britt, o.s.b., rev. ed. (New York, 1924), pp. 55-58.

97/7-13. *With ... cherche*: This passage does not appear in C.

101/14-102/5. *Sche ... hym*: This passage appears to be an expansion of the same observation by St. Bernard in his first sermon on Christmas Eve: "licet enim parvulus, sed plenus gratia et veritate, et in quo habitat omnis plenitudo divinitatis corporaliter" (4, 1, *P.L.*, 183, col. 100).

101/18-19. *vertue ... no3t alle be wastede*: C reads: "et quomodo omnipotens uirtus dei corpusculum ne totum dissiparetur contineret."

102/3-4. *was alle hoole schewede*: C has: "tota erat insinuata"; S has: "tota erat infusa." It seems probable that the correct writing was "schowede," a regular northern dialect form for "shoved," with signification of "thrust," "pushed." See OED "shove," v.

103/3. *mouede so faste in the crosse*: C: "mouebatur in cruce"; S: "moriebatur."

103/16. *ande alle made love*: Not in C or S.

103/18-19. *whiche ... alle*: C reads: "que me omnibus amabilem et sociabilem ac mirabilem faciebat." Version S has "imitabilem" instead of "mirabilem."

104/14-15. *ande thyne blessede werkes into alle the worldys*: The *Booke* reflects C's error: "et opera beata in secula seculorum." S reads: "et operabitur in saecula saeculorum."

105/12-13. *Sche sawe also Saynte Iohan*: The appearance of St. John is frequent in mystical revelations. Cf. *Revelations of Mechthild of Magdeburg*, trans. L. Menzies, p. 118, and the biography of St. Lutgarde, *What Are These Wounds?* by Thomas Merton (Milwaukee, 1950), p. 19.

106/16. *a chaleys*: This image might be occasioned by St. Bernard's exposition of St. John's "will" of martyrdom; the apostle accepted the chalice of salvation offered by the Lord. *In Nativitate SS. Innocentium*, 1, *P.L.*, 183, col. 130. See Note 109/13.

107/15. *lyght of the godhede*: This is probably scribal error in mistaking "lyght" for "height." C has "diuine altitudinis."

108/14. *karolle*: This word is used here and at 274/5 to describe celestial processions and dances. The ambiguities and confusions of meanings associated with the word are examined in the Introduction to *The Early English Carols*, ed. Richard Leighton Greene (Oxford, 1935). Mr. Greene points out that in the fifteenth century carols were beginning to identify songs that could be sung with or without dancing, but in the North the older meaning, ring-dance with accompanying song, was still retained (p. xx). See too by the same author, *A Selection of English Carols* (Oxford, 1962), pp. 1-12. There is no question but that movement is described here; C has "coream." In Mechtild of Magdeburg's visions heavenly Dances of Praise are described, *Revelations*, pp. 21, 231; the editor notes that the mystic dance of the soul dates from pre-Christian times (p. xxviii). Henry Suso, *The Life of the Servant*, trans. James M. Clark (London, 1952), pp. 29-30, also heard celestial music and was invited to dance with the angels.

109/13. *he dranke venym*: This refers to the incident incorporated in the legends about St. John; at Ephesus the high priest of the idolators challenged St. John to drink poison as a test of the power of God. The story appears in *The Golden Legend of Jacobus de Voragine*, trans. Granger Ryan and Helmut Ripperger (New York, 1948), p. 61. The incident is often symbolized in art by the chalice and serpent.

109/15. *homlynesse*: The term is used in the *Booke* to describe the quality of personal relationship with God (243/15, 281/11, "hamelye dowȝtere" 486/11). James Walsh in "God's Homely Loving," *The Month*, N.S. 19 (1958) 164-72, discusses the homeliness of God's presence in the revelations of Julian of Norwich. He calls attention to the implied similarity between Julian and St. John Evangelist on the doctrine of the Divine indwelling.

109/20-21. *delyuerede ... dysese*: Another popular legend associated with St. John: as an old man of 99 years he prepared himself for death and disappeared from the earth in a blaze of light (*The Golden Legend*, p. 63). Mechtild of Magdeburg had a vision of the uncorrupted body of St. John lying "in great bliss, above all passing things" (*Revelations*, p. 118).

111/16. *Anni...*: Psal. 101: 28.

111/17-19. *Þarefore ... herte*: Eccli. 24: 26; Matt. 11: 28.

112/1. *is of a wyfe...*: This comparison is one of a varied and extensive catalogue of similitudes employed throughout the work. Sr. Mary Jeremy in her study "Similitudes in the Writing of Saint Gertrude of Helfta," *Mediaeval Studies*, 19 (1957), 48-54, has grouped the imagery of St. Gertrude into five classifications which afford some intriguing glimpses into medieval life and manners. Since St. Gertrude is reputed to be the author, in part at least, of the *Liber* it is not surprising that some manifestations of a like variety and color appear therein. Henry Suso also alludes to the custom of courtly youths requesting bouquets of their ladies for the New Year; the practice was to sing songs and recite poems. Suso requests a New Year's bouquet of grace from the Blessed Virgin after singing her praises. *The Life of the Servant*, pp. 33-35.

113/2. *circumcide*: Joseph E. Milosh, *"The Scale of Perfection" and the English Mystical Tradition* (Madison, Milwaukee, and London, 1966), pp. 194-5, n. 7, in referring to Rolle's term "circumsysede gastely" says it is a traditional metaphor used appropriately "to characterize the lack of contamination in the singular desire for Jesus." He then points out that the allegorical meaning of circumcision is clear in Rabanus Maurus and is further explicated by Alanus de Insulis. St. Bernard's sermon on the Circumcision urges his hearers to perform spiritual circumcisions; Sermo 3, *P.L.*, 183, cols. 138-42.

114/12. *responce*: 2 Lesson of First Nocturn.

114/14. *in a rede cloth*: This follows C's "coctinea ueste." The correct reading is in S "nivea veste."

115/1. *Lorde...*: Matt. 3: 14. For the association of St. John Baptist with the feast of the Epiphany see *The Golden Legend*, p. 84, and St. Bernard's sermon on the Epiphany 1, *P.L.*, 183, cols. 145-46.

115/16. *Ipsum...*: Matt. 17: 5.

115/21. *Venite...*: Matt. 11: 28.

116/2. *Beati...*: Matt. 5: 8.

116/5. *Qui...*: Joann. 6: 55.

116/7. *Qui...*: Joann. 8: 12.

116/11. *Hoc...*: Joann. 15: 12.

116/15. *In...*: Matt. 7: 2.

116/18. *Qui...*: Luc. 14: 27.

117/16-19. On the symbolic meanings of the gifts of the Magi, see St. Bernard's Epiphany sermon 2: 1; 3: 5, *P.L.*, 183, cols. 147-8, 151.

118/5. *In...*: Introit, 1 Sunday after Epiphany.

118/15. *effecte*: The *Booke* shows C's misreading "effectus." S has "affectio."

120/18. *Fadere...*: Psal. 87: 17.

122/1. *Omnis...*: Introit, 2 Sunday after the Epiphany, the feast in honor of the Face of Christ, also called the Veronica. This solemn station was instituted by Innocent III (1198-1216) to be held at the hospital of the Holy Ghost in Rome. The famous relic of the "sudarium Salvatoris" was carried by the pope in solemn procession; the pontiff also preached on the occasion and in addition composed a prayer for the feast to which he attached an indulgence. See Rev. Horace K. Mann, *The Lives of the Popes in the Middle Ages*, 2nd. ed., 18 vols. (London, 1902-32), 11: 87-88.

122/7-8. *iaspere ... golde ... rede stone*: The mainstream of medieval lapidaries had its source in the accounts produced by St. Isidore of Seville in the seventh century and Marbode, bishop of Rennes, in the eleventh century (*English Mediaeval Lapidaries*, edd. Joan Evans and Mary S. Serjeantson [EETS 190, 1933], p. xi). This volume contains the texts of seven manuscripts from the eleventh to the late sixteenth century. Mechtild's symbolic use of precious stones is usually related to their value, color, and beauty (e.g., 272/22-273/10). *The Booke of Gostlye Grace* refers occasionally to the medicinal powers of stones; cf. 325/20, 529/10-12.

122/10. *dignite*: C reads "diuinitatis."

125/17. *go thyddere gostelye*: This refers to the custom of making spiritual pilgrimages.

126/18. *whiche face*: cf. 1 Pet. 1: 12.

128/16. *Saynte Agnes*: The appearance of St. Agnes figures in the visions of St. Lutgarde (Merton, *What Are These Wounds?* p. 121), and St. Gertrude (Dolan, *St. Gertrude*, p. 149). In *The Life of the Servant*, pp. 19-20, Henry Suso relates how one of his early spiritual ecstasies occurred on the feast of St. Agnes.

129/9. *Amo Cristum*: This responsory is the subject of a meditation by St. Gertrude, *Exercises*, p. 44.

129/13-14. *goode holye wordes*: See *The Golden Legend*, pp. 110-11; the words are spoken by St. Agnes as she spurns the gifts of a prefect's son.

133/2. *Quicumque...*: Matt. 12: 50.

133/10-11. *I haffe worscheppede virgyns*: Lofty regard for virginity was evidenced in the early Church, but even in the first centuries the expression of respect grew in volume and intensity to culminate in St. Methodius' unrestrained praise and ascription of honor superior even to that of martyrdom. See Sr. M. Rosamond Nugent, *Portrait of the Consecrated Woman in Greek Christian Literature of the First Four Centuries*, Patristic Studies 64 (1941), diss. (Catholic University of America). One portion of this study examines the symbolic treatment of virginity; the virgin as a censer is an early representation (p. 97). The *Booke* contains a number of compliments to virgins; see 272/11-12, 280/6-281/13, 396/11-397/6, 398/4-5.

134/18-19. *sche schalle sowne*: Since C has "apparebit" and "sound" (OED v[1]) is recorded in the sense of appearing to have a certain signification only when heard or read (not seen), it is probable that the word was originally written "seme."

135/10. *masse*: Feast of St. Agnes.

135/11. *Offerentur*: This word is the former use; now the Offertory begins with "Afferentur" (*Revelationes*, 2: 37, n. 1).

136/20. *Purificacion*: Blessed Henry Suso recounts a vision on the Feast of the Purification wherein the Virgin allows him to carry the Christ Child (*The Life of the Servant*, p. 38).

137/16. *transfygurede*: C reads "transfigurata fuisset"; S has "transfusa fuisset."

137/19. *Tuam...*: Luc. 2: 35.

138/13. *Hec...*: According to the Benedictine editor (*Revelationes*, 2: 38, n. 1) this antiphon was sung during Matins on the feast of the Purification at Helfta.

138/16. *psalme*: 84.

138/17-18. *aungels ... sange þat antymme*: Mechtild hears heavenly choristers elsewhere in her visions (e.g., 153/3). Robert Moore in "The Tradition of Angelic Singing in English Drama," JEGP, 22 (1923), 89-99, points out that the tradition appears to have started in the Middle Ages. See Miss Allen on the subject: *Margery Kempe*, p. 260, n. 11/13-14.

139/17-18. *lyke vermeloune ... stones*: C reads "quasi auro et lapidibus preciosis erant vermiculata."

142/17. *Sondaye*: Quinquagesima Sunday.

143/3. *ane hye hille*: This is the first of several analogies between Dante's *Divine Comedy* and Mechtild's revelations which are advanced as evidence by those who claim Mechtild as the original for Donna Matelda. Three candidates who bear the same name have been suggested as the actual Matilda: the Countess Matilda of Tuscany, Mechtild of Magdeburg, and Mechtild of Hackeborn. The first, a mature and warlike woman, was speedily disposed of as too far removed from the young and gentle paragon of Christian life. As the evidence is not conclusive for either Mechtild, the field is left to both to dispute the honor. Their revelations show striking similarities to passages in the *Divine Comedy* (Gardner lists the analogies, *Dante and the Mystics*, pp. 265-97), and there is reason to believe that both accounts were brought to Italy probably by Dominicans before 1300, the assumed date of Dante's vision. (The Dominican Friars of Halle were longtime friends of Mechtild of Magdeburg and were the neighbors and spiritual directors for the convent at Helfta. Boccaccio's *Decameron*, composed 1353, in the first story of the seventh day, refers to the praises of the Lady Matilda; cf. Note 191/10-194/6.) Champions are not wanting for either nun. W. Preger (*Geschichte*, 1: 87-88) and J. Ancelet-Hustache (*Mechtilde de Magdebourg*, pp. 358-70) hold for Mechtild of Magdeburg while the editor of the Solesmes text supports Mechtild of Hackeborn (*Revelationes*, 2: vii-xii). Miss Menzies (*Mechtild of Magdeburg*, p. xxii) and E. Gardner lean towards Mechtild of Magdeburg, although the latter speculates that both mystics influenced Dante. Charles Grandgent, *The Ladies of Dante's Lyrics* (Cambridge, Mass., 1917), pp. 40-66, offers as a fourth candidate an anonymous Florentine beauty for whom Dante wrote two elegies. He rejects the two nuns as candidates. The conclusion is that absolute identification appears to be impossible.

The use of a mountain divided into seven levels corresponding to the vices and virtues is a traditional scheme. Dante in the *Divine Comedy* uses the same procedure of gradual purification, but the episodes on each level are elaborated to include interviews with or descriptions of those penitents expiating their sins. Morton Bloomfield in *The Seven Deadly Sins* (East Lansing, 1952) has presented a history of the concept of the seven cardinal sins. There is a brief reference to Mechtild's image of the penitential mountain on p. 158.

143/21. *Ryse...*: Cantic. 2: 14.

144/2. *so merylye*: The merriment in heaven is frequently alluded to, but not always in association with the sounds of joyful singing; see "merye fellaschepe of sayntys" (191/1-2), "God ... schewede hym so iokunde ande merye" (199/19-20), "the companye of hevene schalle wondere with a ynwarde myrth ande gladnesse" (508/8-9). See also 360/14, 382/2. Margery Kempe's exclamation: "it is ful mery in Hevyn" (*Book*, 11/16) is occasioned by hearing angel-song.

145/18. *fowre ryuers of waters of lyffe*: Cf. Gen. 2: 10. The four rivers of Paradise: Phison, Gihon, Tigris, and Euphrates were interpreted in medieval exegesis to represent allegorically the rivers of truth flowing from Christ through the Evangelists, or from Moses through the four major prophets; morally the four cardinal virtues; and anagogically the four blessings which irrigate Paradise. (See Hopper, *Medieval Number Symbolism*, p. 111.) In art they were early identified as symbols for the Evangelists: *Symbolism in Liturgical Art*, LeRoy H. Appleton and Stephen Bridges (New York, 1959), pp. 79-80. In one section of the late twelfth-century meditative tract, *De Quadripertito Exercitio Cellae* by Adam of Dryburgh after he became a Carthusian, the rivers betoken the four chief "exercises of the cell": reading, meditation, prayer, and work. See *Eden's Fourfold River*, ed. A Monk of Parkminster (London, 1927), and James Bulloch, *Adam of Dryburgh* (London, 1958), pp. 30 et seq. and 152 et seq.

146/6. *moystere*: Translates "ubertate." Cf. 178/21.

146/13. *God...*: Apoc. 7: 17.

148/3. *respone*: Responsory on the Feast of the Holy Trinity.

148/5. *antyme*: Antiphon for the feast of the Holy Trinity. All the Latin passages in this chapter are from the same feast.

151/12. *hadde awaye*: Elliptical form. C has "abstulit."

153/4. *Iacta...*: Psal. 54: 23.

153/11. *Si...*: Luc. 23: 31.

154/22. *masse tyme*: Tuesday of Holy Week.

155/17. *epistle*: Phil. 2: 9.

157/10-11. *for I conceyue euery creature*: The glossing admits C's meaning: "quia ego contentiuus sum tocius creature," but it is possible that the scribe should have copied "conteyne." See 101/18 where E has "conteyne & be conceueude" for the Latin "continerat," but B writes "conceyue and be conceyuyd." A similar idea is expressed by "conteynes" 245/20.

160/4. *sche thouȝt*: Neither E nor B is literally faithful to C's "innuebatur."

160/6-13. *hitt ... passion*: St. Bernard comments on Christ's joy when men meditate on his Passion, *De Diligendo Deo*, 3, *P.L.*, 182, col. 979.

163/7-8. *ande þan es that wille acceptable*: This theme of God accepting the will for the deed appears elsewhere; see 429/4-6, 544/6, and 553/1-2. The same sentiments expressed in only slightly different wordings appear in *The Cloud of Unknowing* (cf. 139/19-20 and note) and *The Book of Margery Kempe* (cf. 49/20-21, 90/14-15, 212/21 and notes).

164/7-8. *terys for deuocioun of my passioun*: This practice is recommended often. E. Colledge, *Chastising*, pp. 59-60, observes that the devotion of tears was exempt from the reprehensible forms of enthusiasm. See below Note 214/3-215/2.

165/11-12. *my bones ande entreylys myght be nowmbrede*: This torture of the Passion is specifically referred to twice again; see 356/9-11 and 423/5-7. C. Horstman, *Yorkshire Writers*, 1: 206, reprints a meditation lamenting the stretching of Christ's body on the Cross so that all his bones were visible.

165/15. *Cum...*: Joann. 12: 32.

166/12. *Ego...*: 1 Cor. 15: 9-10.

166/18-19. *the crosse schulde be bervede*: This refers to the "depositio crucis," a ceremonial described by Karl Young, *The Drama of the Medieval Church*, 2 vols. (Oxford, 1933), 1: 112-48, in his investigation of liturgical roots of drama. The "depositio" occurs on Good Friday between None and

Vespers; it involves the placement of the Cross in a "sepulchre" in commemoration of the burial of Christ.

166/21. *be thyselfe*: "be" should be "berye." C reads "teipsum sepeli."

167/3-4. *ande the excercyes of alle thy wittes ande dedys*: E shows C's error: "et excercitacio omnium sensuum et actuum tuorum." S: "et exercitatio omnium membrorum motuumque tuorum."

167/17. *here prayers*: This probably refers to Matins. This chapter and the next are arranged around the hours of the Office as reflective of meditations on the Passion. St. Gertrude uses the same scheme in her meditations for the Seventh Exercise; see *Exercises*, pp. 145-73.

169/5. *knawynge*: "of the godhede" should follow. C has "secundum lumen diuine cognicionis."

171/8. *Myne eleccioune mayde me do hitt*: Cf. 71/4-11. This is the first of some explicit assertions of "election." See 365/4-5 for another application to Mechtild's salvation and 519/4-8 for reference to a sister of the community. Miss Allen (*Book*, p. 271, note 29/22-23) comments on similar expressions by Margery Kempe and a number of German women mystics.

171/22. *lybertey*: C reads "libertas"; S has "liberalitas."

173/9. *gloryouste*: Not in OED. There is one citation in MED ("gloriuste") but its meaning "renown" is not applicable here where the *Liber* has "gloria." The *Booke* invariably translates the Latin word as "glory" or "splendour."

173/10. *wryth*: This is the weak past part. of the strong v. OE "wriðan." B often drops the inflexion in past t. and past part.

173/19. *comwnede*: On Good Friday the faithful received the Sacrament between None and Vespers.

174/19-20. *kysse the crosse*: The "adoratio crucis" is one of the oldest liturgical observances of Holy Week. It took place in the medieval church during the period between None and Vespers, prior to the "depositio" (Young, *The Drama of the Medieval Church*, 1: 117-18).

175/13. *in grete pacyence*: C has "in summa paciencia"; S has "in summe placentia."

176/1-2 *as irene glowynnge with fyre*: This similitude was also used by St. Bernard in *De Diligendo Deo*, 10, *P.L.*, 182, col. 991.

177/4. *myrtiene tree*: E follows C's "oleum mirtinum"; S has "oleum myrrhinum." OED ("myrrh-tree," "myrtine," "myrt-tree") notes that in several manuscripts of the Wycliffite Bible "myrtle" is a variant for "myrrh."

178/3, 8. *vij*: Both C and S read "sexta."

178/8. *Exaltabo...*: Psal. 29.

178/10-11. *as oure lorde suffrede woundeys*: This indirect method of counting Christ's wounds gives a total of 4,732. Note that the variant reading of B (179/3) gives the sum as 5,460. This latter number also appears in a poem entitled Lamentation of St. Mary on the Passion (Horstman, *Yorkshire Writers*, 2: 281). Miss Allen has a lengthy note (*Book of Margery Kempe*, p. 334, n. 191/5-15) demonstrating the popular custom of precisely identifying the number in devotional manuals. Cf. also Horstman, *Yorkshire Writers*, 1: 121. Later on (537/17-19), Mechtild is represented as saying 5,080 Paters in remembrance of Christ's wounds.

178/19. *medycine of sawles*: MED ("medicine," 2b, fig.) lists some combinations with medicine that serve as epithets for God or Christ. The use in the *Booke* here and 183/5 conforms to the theme of Christ's wounds as remedies. See Gray, "The Five Wounds of Our Lord," pp. 127-30.

178/21. *þe watere of lyfe ande wyne of gostely moystour*: C reads "aqua viuificans et vinum inebrians."

181/3-5. *awngels ... as a walle*: The image of crowds of angels as thick as a wall occurs often; see 80/15, 81/6, 219/16-17, and 331/13. *Speculum Devotorum* (248/10-14) alludes to this description of the heavenly hosts at the sepulchre. See above, p. 50, item 12.

182/7. *When the sepulcre schulde be vysitede*: Young, *Drama of the Medieval Church*, 1: 239-410, discusses the extra-liturgical custom of the "visitatio sepulchri" on Easter morning.

183/18. *wodde of cedre*: St. Bernard, *Sermones in Cantica Canticorum*, 18, *P.L.* 183, cols. 1004-05, refers to the lofty cedar with its imperishable fragrant wood.

186/14. *Resurexi*: Introit, Easter Sunday.

187/19. *processioun*: Only four processions were prescribed in Cistercian houses: on Palm Sunday, Ascension, Purification, and Assumption. Archdale A. King, *Liturgies of the Religious Orders* (Milwaukee, 1955), p. 131.

187/22. *dalmaticke or a tunacle*: Originally two separate garments, in time they differed little in appearance and the terms were often used interchangeably. The dalmatic was adopted as a vestment for deacons by the twelfth century; the tunicle was given at ordination during the fourteenth or fifteenth centuries. See King, *Liturgy of the Roman Church*, pp. 133-7.

188/16. *Regina celi*: One of the four Antiphons of the Blessed Virgin. In the present liturgy it is sung from Compline of Holy Saturday until None of the Saturday after Pentecost. The earliest text of this hymn is from the beginning of the thirteenth century; see Herbert Thurston, s.J., "The Regina Caeli," *Familiar Prayers: Their Origin and History* (Westminster, 1953), pp. 146-51.

188/18. *trefoyles ande bryght scheldys*: The trefoil, a familiar emblem of the Trinity, is a modification of the three interlaced circles which traditionally represented the doctrine of the equality of the Three Persons. The shield of the

Trinity was figured in stained glasses of medieval churches in a number of variations; usually three bands of writing represented the sides connecting a circle at each corner. See F. R. Webber, *Church Symbolism*, 2nd ed. (Cleveland, 1938), pp. 43-44.

189/12. *in the euenetyde; in this nyght*: Not in the Latin. C: "Quinque enim fercula in hac cena ministrare uolo."

191/6-10. *Aftere ... sayde*: This introduction to Mechtild's prayer is not in the *Liber*.

191/10-194/6. *O god Ihesu ... euermore*: This is the prayer by Mechtild that the Solesmes editor identifies as the one Boccaccio said was known in Florence during Dante's time, *Revelationes*, 2: 65, n. 1. See also Note 143/3.

193/2-3. *and bowe ... to me*: C: "et placa michi deum patrem iudicem equissimum."

193/20. *Volo...*: Joann. 17: 24.

196/11. *Mane...*: Luc. 24: 29.

199/7. *without a thorne*: The emendation based on C is necessary: "En ego rosa sine spina natus multis spinis sum punctatus." In the Middle Ages the older Christian association of the rose with the blood of martyrs and Christ survived, but the rose came to be related far more often with the Virgin in sermons, tracts, and hymns. See Woolf, *English Religious Lyric*, pp. 287-8. The "roose withowtyne thorne" expression is applied to the Virgin 261/20-21.

199/14. *he toke here be the handdys*: This vision has a parallel in the Lord's promise to take Margery Kempe by the hand and dance with her in heaven. *Book*, 52/27-29.

203/17-18. *Qui...*: Eph. 4: 10.

205/21. *representede ... hymselfe*: i.e., Christ presented to the Father in his own person.

207/16. *Ysaie*: 11: 2, 3.

208/15. *euerelastyng*: This is C's "eternam," not S's "internam."

211/2. *Omnis ... domini*: 2 Lesson, Matins.

211/9. *Et ... eos*: 3 Antiphon, Lauds.

211/10. *sche sawe a hande...*: In medieval art, a hand emerging from a cloud of glory making the gesture of benediction with thumb and first two fingers extended represented God the Father and signified Divine intervention. Mâle, *The Gothic Image*, p. 2; Webber, *Church Symbolism*, pp. 49-50.

212/2. *Infirmitatem nostram*: These words are from the Collect of the Mass of a Martyr Bishop.

212/9. *brothere of lyons*: Cf. Job 30: 29.

212/13. *fulle hy*: C has "superna"; S reads "fraterna."

214/3-215/2. *Apon ... kepede*: The substance of this chapter on the virtue of tears is repeated frequently; see 164/7-8, 358/18-20, 492/11-12. Note that in the catalogue of Mechtild's moral excellences special attention is given to her tears (602/20, 604/21). St. Bernard's sermon on the Epiphany, 3, *P.L.* 183, col. 152, grades tears in the ascending order of contrition, devotion, and compassion.

214/3. *gospelle*: Joann. 11: 35.

216/7. *Ego...*: Psal. 81: 6.

218/7, 8. *his owne luffe; his bodylye luffe*: Both readings are correct if they mean "self-love." It is possible that they are misreadings for "lyffe." C reads "quod suimet oblivionem pereat" [S: "pariat"].

219/8. *tracte*: Vigil of Pentecost (*Revelationes*, 2: 79, n. 1).

220/17. *fro oure lordys herte*: The well or fountain theme as applied to Christ is very old and was early associated with the devotion to the Precious Blood and the Wounded Side. Later in the *Booke* the Lord is seen in procession to the font of baptism with a stream of redemptive water flowing from his heart (222/3-223/5); Mechtild sees the Trinity as a "fons vivus" (229/9-230/4); Christ's heart is a well of goodness (329/23, 429/18-19). See Gray, "The Five Wounds of Our Lord," p. 132, n. 44.

221/10. *Rex sanctorum*: Litany sung on the Saturday before Pentecost (*Revelationes*, 2: 80, n. 1).

222/20. *heuens of heuens*: the highest heaven (MED).

225/3. *Ionatha*: See 1 Sam. 19: 2. *swolwyde*: The translator has confused "conglutinare" with "gluttire." C correctly reads "conglutinate" here; "swolwynge of luffe" (225/5) translates "glutino amoris."

227/1-2. *Tibi...*: Offertory of Whitsunday.

227/11. *eernese*: Miss Allen in her notes to the *Book of Margery Kempe*, p. 265, n. 18/3, contrasts Richard Rolle's and Hilton's uses of the term, "ernest-peny." Rolle uses "arra" to express the sweetness granted to contemplatives on earth. Hilton is cautious about its permanence and very skeptical about its existence.

228/5. *Veni creator...*: This invocation to the Holy Spirit is of uncertain authorship, having been ascribed to Rabanus Maurus, Charlemagne, St. Ambrose, and St. Gregory the Great (Britt, *Hymns of the Breviary*, p. 163).

229/19-21. *and ʒit ... nowʒt fayllede*: Translates "et tamen in se indeficiens."

232/14. *here sustere ... abbesse*: Gertrude von Hackeborn.

233/7. *Incorupcio...*: Sap. 6: 20.

234/11. *Fides...*: Luc. 7: 50.

235/18. *Þyne synnys...*: Luc. 7: 48, 50.

239/8. *Throny*: This plural form is seen again: "throni" (317/9); elsewhere it is "thronys" (169/7, 268/12).

239/17-18. *Vertues ... mye worschepe*: Translates "virtutes in cumulum honoris mei."

241/18. *cherelye*: No adj. form in MED or OED. The word was probably incorrectly written in the parent manuscript of E and B. C reads "blandissimo affectu." See Note 524/8.

243/18-19. *desyrede God more preciouslye*: A literal rendering of C "deum preciosius desiderans"; S correctly reads "Dominum prae omnibus desiderans."

245/13. *Salue*: This entire Responsory appears in *Revelationes*, 2: 92, n. 1.

246/5. *as a sperkelle*: Miss Hodgson (*Cloud of Unknowing*, p. 187, note 22/8) calls attention to the same simile used in the *Scale of Perfection* and the *Benjamin Major*.

246/16. *þe ioyes of oure ladye*: The formula of devotion that follows concentrates on meditation. Usually specific prayers are prescribed. See Sitwell's note on the Five Joys in *The Ancrene Riwle*, pp. 195-6. Later on 260/3-261/22, the Blessed Virgin recommends the recitation of Aves in recollection of three joys she has in the knowledge of the Trinity.

247/16. *vnmesurabylite*: The macron over the first *e* in this word might signify "—mensur—," derived from L. "mensurabilis," but the more usual stem in ME is "—mesur—" based on Fr. "mesurable." MED records both "immensurable" and "immesurable" in the fifteenth century, but E's form is not listed in either MED or OED. "Immensurability" and "immeasurability" are cited in OED examples dated 1675 and 1824 respectively.

248/2. *reboundynge*: Translates "redundancia." In ME "rebound" was often confused with "redound." See OED "rebound" v.

251/6-8. *clene ... charyte*: C reads "dulcia inuicem uerba et charitatiua opera."

251/17-21. It was probably during the 1290s that the interdict was imposed on the convent. There does not seem to be any specific evidence about its cause or its duration. Allusions in Mechtild's and St. Gertrude's writings and brief references in other records suggest that certain canons usurped the functions of the bishop of Halberstadt, in whose diocese the monastery was situated, and demanded revenues from the convent. The canons pronounced an interdict against the nuns forbidding them to chant the Office or to have Mass said in the convent choir until the difficulty was resolved. See *Revelationes*, 1: 143-9; Dolan, *St. Gertrude the Great*, pp. 32-33.

252/8. *processioun*: See Note 187/19.

252/9. *Vidi...*: 1 Lesson, 1 Nocturn, Feast of the Assumption.

253/5. *as bryght as þe lyght of þe sunne*: Cf. Introit for the Assumption: "Signum magnum apparuit in caelo: mulier amicta sole, et luna sub pedibus eius, et in capite eius corona stellarum duodecim."

254/1-2. *offrede ryngges of golde*: See Note 409/9-10.

254/13-14. *lyftede vppe þe ooste*: The elevation of the host became standard practice in Cistercian monasteries during the thirteenth century. King, *Liturgies*, p. 134.

255/2. *qwele*: C: "fistula"; see Note 76/20-21.

255/3-4. *alle þaye sowkede*: Miss Allen's note on a similar expression in Margery Kempe's *Book* (pp. 264-5, 18/2), points out that the experience was paralleled by some Continental women mystics. She also refers to Dame Julian's association of the image with the reception of the Eucharist. See *The Revelations of Divine Love*, trans. James Walsh, s.j. (New York, 1961), p. 164.

257/12. *as companye*: Based on C's error "ut velut conventus"; S has "ut velut cum ventus."

258/4. *stole of glorye*: See the Alleluia of the Mass of a Doctor: "stolam gloriae induit eum."

261/6. *Ludens...*: Prov. 8: 30; epistle of the Feast of the Nativity of the Blessed Virgin.

262/7. *þame*: B's folio 46ʳ ends with this word ("hem") and is followed by some cancelled ones. A partially legible rubric is in the lower margin: "The summe of the Auees ys thys moche"; several Roman digits, some cancelled, follow.

263/8. *fulle fayre tree*: This vision of the Virgin is inspired by the exegesis of Isai. 11: 1. St. Ambrose interpreted the root of Jesse as the family of the Jews, the stem as Mary, and the flower of the stem as Christ. (Cf. also Rom. 15: 12.) The mirror is a universal symbol for the Blessed Virgin (cf. Sap. 8: 26). See Appleton and Bridges, *Symbolism in Liturgical Art*, pp. 51, 64.

263/18. *Aue preclara*: A hymn by the Benedictine monk, Hermannus Contractus, for the feast of the Assumption. The next three Latin passages are excerpted. See *Analecta Hymnica Medii Aevi* 50 (1907), pp. 313-14.

268/7. *Delicie...*: Prov. 8: 31.

268/9. *Inambulabo...*: 2 Cor. 6: 16.

270/7. *inclynes*: Genuflections were unknown at this time; the custom was to perform a profound inclination. King, *Liturgies*, p. 135.

271/20-21. *I schalle aunswere fullye for the in alle thyngges*: The theme of Christ perfecting man's imperfections is a frequently repeated motif in these revelations. It occurs by implication, by petition, and by affirmation. See 75/22, 119/1, 157/9, 172/9, 277/9, 341/20, 351/3 etc.

273/11. *Ora...*: Versicle of Matins, used at Helfta on the feast of All Saints (*Revelationes*, 2: 105, n. 1).

273/19. *trefolde corde*: Dom Dolan (*St. Gertrude the Great*, p. 125 n.) observes that this motif is symbolic of mutual affection. The twisted cord was a common heraldic device and is often seen surrounding the coat of arms of abbeys or monasteries.

275/1. *Ibi...*: The Antiphon appears in *Revelationes*, 2: 106, n. 1.

275/3. *Laudate...*: Psal. 150: 4.

275/13. *Incorupcio...*: Sap. 6: 20.

277/16-17. *curyouse craftye grauynge*: The high altar in Cistercian churches was originally a simple table on columns; a retable or reredos was forbidden. In 1259 the general chapter ordered the abbot of Royaumont to remove the "novelties"; these were the pictures, curtains, sculptures, and columns with angels which the king had donated to the church. See King, *Liturgies*, p. 119.

278/3. *thre grees*: Durandus, in Book 1 of his *Rationale*, 37-38, also sees the steps to the altar as symbolic of the ascent of virtues.

279/9. *a pousande sawlys...*: One of Mechtild of Magdeburg's visions (*Revelations*, pp. 38-39) relates how Christ promised the ex-beguine the release of 1,000 souls from Purgatory for her tears of love. The "deuoute sustere" (279/6) might refer to this elderly visionary.

280/1, 7. *awrealle blysse...*; *aureale ioye...*: These compound terms translate C's "aureolae (omnium virginum beatarum)" and "aureola (beate uirginis)."

280/6-281/13. This passage comprises the lengthiest praise of virgins and virginity in the revelations; see Note 133/10-11.

280/7. See Note 280/1.

282/11. *sprynggynge welle*: C: "fontem viuus." For the image of the flowing well, cf. Zach. 13: 1.

284/10. *whelys of golde*: The embroidered wheels signify the instrument on which St. Catherine was tortured. The wheel usually appears with the saint in artistic representations.

284/14. *Aue...*: This responsory is listed by Ulysse Chevalier, *Repertorium Hymnologicum*, 1: 132.

285/9. *onys comwnede*: A passage omitted in C should properly follow this phrase. It is in S: "decorem illum in anima sua duplicavit. Qui vero centies aut millies communicaverit, ..."

285/14. *Laudate...*: Psal. 116.

286/8. *sequence*: The entire sequence appears in *Revelationes*, 2: 111, n. 1.

286/21. ʒ*alowe*: Translates "glaucos" (C, S).

287/6-7. *ande for ... techynge*: The translation tries to make a reasonable reply from C's "quia adhuc a parentibus nutritus eram." S has "quia ad hoc a parentibus nutritus eram."

288/8. *Qui...*: Matt. 16: 24.

292/3. *replenschynge*: Earliest example of this verbal noun in the OED is 1528.

293/19. *Deus...*: Gradual of the Mass for the feast of a dedication of a church.

294/6-7. *of precious stonys ande lyuynge sayntis*: C reads "ex lapidibus preciosis et viuis scilicet sanctis...."

297/21. *teyne*: This verb might have been glossed as a form of "tente" (cf. 433/6); OED ("tent," v.¹) records the variant "teynt." But "teen" is a variant of "tend" (OED, v.¹) and E shows the loss of "d" in the environment of "n" in "Wennesdaye" 31/7.

298/14. *in here lyffe*: C reads "inuita."

300/20-21. *Be þe feete ... affeccions*: This passage does not appear in C, but other references to feet on 423/8-11, 426/1-2, 440/11-12, 573/16-17 do follow the *Liber*. In medieval exegesis, the foot often stood for "affectus" or "affectiones." Wenzel, *The Sin of Sloth*, p. 65, remarks that this is "not a matter of sentiment and 'feeling' but of will and love resulting in 'good works' "; he also points (p. 237) to the interpretation of "affectus" or "affectiones" for "pes" in authors ranging from Alanus of Lille to Wyclif and suggests that it is derived from Augustine. Miss Hodgson in her edition of *The Cloud of Unknowing and The Book of Privy Counselling* comments on the image in these works (notes to 14/13-14, 112/14, 146/28). *The Orcherd of Syon*, edd. Phyllis Hodgson and Gabriel Liegey (EETS 258, 1966), pp. 197/22-23, reads "For þere ben two feet of affeccioun, by þe whyche boþe þe preceptis and þe counceylis ben obserued and kepte...."

303/4. *slugerye ande slewth*: Translates "tepor et accidia." "Slugerye" is not recorded under "sluggardy" in the OED.

304/4. *Cum...*: Psal. 17: 26.

306/21. *Þe refute of alle poure*: This follows C's wording: "refugium omnium pauperum." S reads "... peccatorum."

307/10-11. *Aftere this ... vij poyntis*: C reads "Post hec datum est ei salutare cor uirginis gloriose in hijs septem articulis...."

310/8. *Satterdaye*: Dom Gougaud, *Dévotions et pratiques*, ch. 4, examines the tradition of Saturdays consecrated to the Blessed Virgin, and recounts some legends purporting to demonstrate that the day is of special significance to Mary. The origin is unknown but the actual liturgical usage of the Office of Saturdays dedicated to the Virgin has been traced to the second half of the tenth century. (Ibid., p. 69.)

310/11. *pleysynge salutacioun*: Fr. Thurston in "The Origins of the *Hail Mary*," *Familiar Prayers*, pp. 90-114, reviews the complicated history of the Ave Maria, and traces its beginnings back to the words of the angel Gabriel as recited in the Little Office of the Blessed Virgin. By the eleventh century the greeting came to be used as an independent formula of salutation, and was developed into the form used in these revelations before the end of the twelfth century.

313/6-7. *ande þat sche lettede neuere hereselfe in hereselfe*: She never hindered it in herself. C: "nec unquam eam in se impediuit."

315/11-12. *to brynge to me synfulle men*: Later, the Blessed Virgin is called "mediatrice betwyxte God and mane" (369/18).

325/12. *commemoracion*: C's "memoria" is supplied.

326/23. *rede rosys*: The *Booke* as well as C omits the golden roses woven over the red roses. S reads "Maria habebat amictum crocei coloris, in quo erant rosae rubeae et in ipsis rosae aureae mirabiliter intextae." Cf. 327/5-7.

327/1. *fulle worschepfullye*: Translates "mirabiliter intextae."

328/16-19. *Ande howe ... betokenede*: These sentences do not appear in the Table of Chapters. See 26/4.

329/1. *Asperges...*: Psal. 50: 9.

329/14. *pystelle*: Galat. 5: 22.

330/2. *syonys of the vyne*: The translator seems to be substituting the common figure of Christ as a vine. C has "palmites."

331/17. *Miserere...*: Psal. 50.

331/20. *O beata...*: Antiphon of the former Office of the Blessed Trinity (*Revelationes*, 2: 138, n. 1).

334/15. *duche tonge*: See above, pp. 12-14, for a discussion of the German and English interpolations at this point in some versions of the *Liber*.

334/16-19. *The substance ... dowhttere*: This passage appears in English in C, see p. 13 above.

335/9. *brydde*: This follows C's "auis." S reads "apis."

337/6-10. *ande so ... lessone*: C reads "eam circumplectens et ad se trahens a quo cum magna difficultate et penalitate se erexit et uix lectionem legere poterat."

339/15. *sengynge*: C has "coquens." The word gave both English scribes trouble. E seems to have interpreted it as "singe" (to burn); B reads "seethe" (to boil). Perhaps the original English text referred to the "singing" of boiling water.

340/19. *the terynge of his berde*: Cf. "It is to be read in a certain writing that the Lord revealed to one of His devoted ones that His head was shorn and His beard torn"; in the latest English version of *Meditations on the Life of Christ*, trans. from an Italian manuscript by Isa Ragusa and Rosalie B. Green (Princeton, 1961), p. 342. In a recent article Edmund Colledge, o.s.a., "Dominus cuidam devotae suae: a Source for Pseudo-Bonaventure," *Franciscan Studies*, 36/Annual xiv (1976), 105-107, points out the strong probability that "one of His devoted ones" is Mechtild and the "certain writing" is the *Liber*. If this is so, he concludes, it means that the *Meditations* cannot have been composed before 1300, thus ruling out St. Bonaventure not only as author of that work but also as editor of the *Meditationes de Passione Christi* recension.

341/15. *fyfty ʒere*: Mechtild was fifty years old in 1290 or 1291.

345/12. *drede of hevynesse*: C reads "immittens cordi eius timorem illum et tristiciam."

350/3. *Confirmatum...*: Responsory of 5 Lesson, Matins, feast of the Circumcision.

352/17. *fulle herde fruyte*: Both C and S have "dulcissimum fructum."

353/12. *nempne thy modere onlye in me*: This maternal view of the love of God was not unusual during the Middle Ages. Its roots are in the Old Testament, especially in Deuteronomy, Isaias, and Jeremias wherein the Fatherhood of God is often demonstrated in terms associated with motherhood: tender, protective, cherishing, unchangeable. In ancient Christianity the name of Mother is rarely used, but the maternal love of the Godhead is referred to in some Eastern commentaries. In the West the devotion became pronounced with St. Anselm who addressed Jesus as Mother in Prayer 65. It was fostered probably by the wide diffusion of St. Anselm's writings and received expression in the works of mystics of the twelfth and thirteenth centuries. Dominic of Treves, a fifteenth-century Carthusian, refers to both Christ and the Holy Ghost as our Mother. The classic exposition of the Motherhood of God occurs in the *Revelations* of Julian of Norwich. The Divine Motherhood is grounded in the Being of God, but Julian applies it especially to Christ, being careful in no way to detract from the honor and dignity accorded to the role of the Blessed Mother. S.M.A., o.p., " 'God is Our Mother,' " *Blackfriars*, 26 (1945), 49-53; André Cabassut, o.s.b., "Une dévotion médiévale peu connue—La dévotion à 'Jésus notre mère'," *Revue d'ascétique et de mystique*, 98-100 (1949), 234-45. Cf. 436/15.

354/13. *lovynglye*: The only use of this as an adj. is recorded in OED in an example dated 1567.

357/10-11. *nootede in hereselfe*: Cf. St. Bernard's description of mystical union in *De Diligendo Deo*, 10, *P.L.* 182, col. 990: "Te enim quodammodo perdere, tanquam qui non sis et omnino non sentire teipsum, et a teipso exinaniri, et pene anullari...."

358/13. *Laudate...*: Psal. 148.

361/2. *Os...*: Psal. 118: 131.

363/6-7. *Ande to conferme ... sykernesse*: This statement, part of the rubric for the next chapter (364/14-15), is misplaced here and also in C and T.

364/8. *within me*: This phrase is an excrescence. C reads "infra te quoque firmamentum tenens animam ['meam' cancelled] tuam."

366/18. *Cetus...*: From the hymn "Gloria, laus, et honor," a processional hymn on Palm Sunday.

370/7. *presence*: This is C's reading also; S has "providentiae."

371/15. *in lykenes of a peese*: The *Booke* follows C's error "pisi"; S reads "piscis." The fish image occurs often, e.g., 376/7-8, 381/10.

374/15. *Deduc...*: Psal 85: 11.

380/8. *þe þrydde howse*: The translation reflects C's misreading "terciam domum" for "totam domum."

381/4-10. *Wharefore þay ... the eyre*: This confusing passage reflects C's inept combination of materials from two separate paragraphs in the longer *Liber*. C has "Vnde plurimi legacionem suam ad deum ipsi committebant, quibus singulis prout dominus sibi dignabatur ostendere desideria cordis eorum intimabat, ac per hoc plurimum letificati deo gracias retulerunt. Vnde anima eius in diuinitate natabat sicut piscis in aqua et auis in aere." See *Revelationes*, 2: 169-70.

383/4. *wryttene*: Psal. 21: 7.

387/9-13. *When þou erte seke ... in othere tymes*: This revelation contradicts the established tradition of the right side of Christ being more favorable. Dom Gougaud, *Dévotions et pratiques*, pp. 91-97, points out that the wound of the right side was believed to be the way to the Sacred Heart. St. Gertrude is privileged to be placed at the right side of Christ (*Revelationes*, 1: 303). St. Bernard exalts the right hand embrace because he associates it with the Beatific Vision (*De Diligendo Deo*, 3, *P.L.* 182, col. 979-81). Note, however, that Love stands at the right side of God (392/10), and that religious men and women are under the care of the right hand of God (507/9-10).

388/21. *a wyndowe*: Doors and windows usually refer to the bodily senses. See ch. xxxix (401/6-402/20) for the exgesis of the five doors in terms of Christ's humanity.

390/2-3. *so moche ... comprehendyd*: C: "tanto arcius et dulcius incomprehensam meam latitudinem circumcingis."

391/1, 11. *Gyrum...*: *Et in...*: Eccli. 24: 8.

392/15. *In psalterio...*: Psal. 32: 2.

393/3-9. *Te Deum ... gloria*: from the Antiphon of 2 Vespers of Trinity Sunday.

396/21. *Quam...*: Cant. 7: 1.

397/4. *Veni...*: Cant. 4: 8.

399/19-400/1. *whan a mane ... sauoure of God*: C has " cum homo se minus sentit in oracione deuotum amore frigidum et a deo elongatum."

400/12. *Obliuiscere...*: Psal. 44: 11.

401/6-402/20. *Anothere ... children*: This chapter appears as the first part of ch. 8 in Part 1 of the longer *Liber* (*Revelationes*, 2: 26-27).

401/10. *humanyte*: The *Booke*, like C, omits the description of two gates found in S: "Duae autem januae inferiores designabant pedes ejus; quae habebant columnam in medio in qua scriptus erat hic versus: Venite ad me...."

401/11. *Venite...*: Matt. 11: 28.

402/1. *Accipite...*: Introit, Tuesday after Pentecost.

402/13. *Accedite...*: Psal. 33: 6.

403/5-18. This chapter is from Part 1, ch. 9 in the unabridged *Liber* (*Revelationes*, 2: 30).

403/13. *of*: Scribal error for "and."

404/7-406/4. *In ... delicys*: This chapter appears at the end of Part 1, ch. 13 in the unabridged *Liber* (*Revelationes*, 2: 44-45).

405/9. *Ducam...*: Cant. 3: 4.

405/19. *Panem...*: Psal. 77: 25.

406/10. *a persone*: This most probably refers to St. Gertrude; see above, p. 37.

408/18. *Et tibi...*: Introit, Mass for the Dead.

409/9-10. *rynge ... of desponsacion*: All the preceding ceremonies enacted in the heart of Christ culminate in the spiritual espousal described in this chapter. The espousal in turn is reminiscent of the elaborate ritual of the consecration of virgins as performed in the cloister at Helfta. The giving of the ring (409/5) is part of the rite, and elsewhere (503/9) Mechtild reveals how Christ instructed her on renewing her espousal. St. Gertrude's third spiritual exercise, "Espousals and Consecration," details the ceremony (*Exercises*, pp. 27-49). The accompanying (409/17-412/3) rehearsal of Christ's life and Passion in terms of preparations for a wedding harmonizes with the nuptials motif.

409/19. *of my godhede*: This translates C's "diuinitatis mee"; S reads "digiti tui."

413/11. *Delicie...*: Prov. 8: 31.

416/16. *Tibi decus*: This entire prayer appears in *Revelationes*, 2: 201.

419/17-420/12. *als a fadere ... freende ... spowse*: Christ calls Margery Kempe (*Book*, 31/22-23) his daughter, mother, sister, wife, and spouse. Horstman (*Yorkshire Writers*, 1: 368-70) prints a long poem wherein Jesus is addressed as father, mother, brother, sister, and spouse. Elsewhere in these revelations (196/15-197/18) Christ promises to dwell as man's father, friend, spouse, and companion; another time as father, mother, brother, sister (534/17-20); and again Mechtild is reminded that through the Incarnation God was made man's brother, companion, and servant (471/19-20).

420/16-17. *with gladdenesse ande þonkkynges*: The translator views these terms as sonynyms; C reads "cum gratitudine." See ll. 15-16 *gladde þonkkynge herte* for C's "cor gratificans" and Note 69/20.

421/16. *writtene*: 1 Cor. 11: 3.

428/12. *Deus...*: Cf. Deut. 32: 4.

433/6. *tente*: This has been interpreted as the northern and Scottish word (OED, "tent" v.¹) rather than as regular "tend" with unvoicing of final -*d* to -*t*.

436/15, 16. *goode modere*; *goode moders*: These are scribal errors for "godmother" (C "commater"). In both ME manuscripts the words are clearly separated. Occasionally E writes modern "good" with a single vowel (47/12, 191/10, 492/8), but "God" never appears with the double vowel.

441/9. *The eeres...*: See 492/13-15, 505/20, and 510/8 for similar expression associating ears with obedience and meekness.

448/6. *psalme*: Psal. 116.

448/9. *with alle þe partyes*: C reads "cum omnibus partibus"; S reads "cum omnibus operibus."

449/3-5. *This maydene ... here owne partye*: This shows C's erroneous "Tunc illa sue partis memor effecta dixit ad dominum." S's reading is "Tunc illa suae paupertatis memor effecta...."

449/7. *syght ande trowth*: Both words render "fidem" in "quo tibi fidem meam consignarem." "Syght" seems to be a misreading for "plyght."

452/2 *Seynte Powle seyes*: Hebr. 4: 12.

456/6. *his prayer*: This is apparently a misinterpretation of "racionem" in C's "cum racionem suam siue intellectum ad terrenam sapienciam et curiositatem conuertit...."

459/15-17. *O my dere lorde ... thy naame to my herte*: Pronouns in the first sentence have been emended in the interests of sense. C: "Scribe dulcissime domine nomen meum in cor tuum nomenque tuum mellifluum cordi meo per iugem memoriam inscribe."

460/11. *my name in thy herte*: C and S agree: "nomen meum in cor tuum."

461/12. *Hoc...*: Luc. 22: 19.

463/15. *Trahe...*: Cf. Cant. 1: 3.

464/1. *Si...*: Joann. 12: 32.

464/7. *thre oyntementis*: St. Bernard, *In Cantica*, 10.6.7, *P.L.* 183, col. 821-2, discusses three ointments appropriate for the Bride of Christ: contrition, devotion, and piety.

466/1-17. *Anothere tyme ... thidere yn*: Here in the midst of a series of chapters (456/2-469/4) on the proper preparation, disposition, and reception of Holy Communion the explicit recommendation is made for frequent receiving of the Eucharist. There seems to be no definite information about what constituted the ordinary practice. See Joseph Duhr, "Communion fréquente," *Dictionnaire de spiritualité ascétique et mystique* (Paris, 1953), vol. 2, pt. 2, col. 1234-91. St. Gertrude and Mechtild are given special mention (col. 1262) for their activity in urging more frequent Communions. It would seem that the religious at Helfta received the Sacrament about twice weekly (Dolan, *St. Gertrude the Great*, p. 39). Other recommendations in the revelations of Mechtild are on 249/21-251/2, 285/5-10, and 579/1-14.

467/10-11. *as two wyndes ... on eyre*: C: "sicut duo uenti insimul flantes vnum aerem spirant."

468/3. *Sine...*: Joann. 15: 5.

470/8. *peynfulle*: The meaning is suffering with pain through mortification. C: "crucifigas tibi mundum teque mundo."

471/21. *Non veni...*: Cf. Matt. 20: 28.

473/21. *profetable*: This form is used again as a quasi-adv. on 515/4-5, 564/16. OED lists only one similar usage, dated 1654.

474/1. *saye ententlye ande deuoutlye*: St. Bernard exhorted his monks to proper recitation and chanting of the Divine Office "pure semper ac strenue" (*In Cantica*, 47, *P.L.* 183, col. 1011).

475/2. *Deus...*: Luc. 18: 13.

477/12. *Occuli...*: *Revelationes*, 2: 238, identifies this as a hymn used during Compline at that time.

480/1, 10. *Propter...*; *Ponam...*: Psal. 11: 6.

481/12-17. *Than sayde ... a sowlle*: In the correct Latin version the Lord asks a purely rhetorical question. In C, Mechtild becomes the questioner. The *Booke* supplies a response.

484/12. *Vnxit...*: Psal. 44: 8.

484/20. *Amice...*: Matt. 22: 12.

485/15-16. *with a sympille herte*: C has "supplici corde."

486/7. *messe*: Last Sunday after Pentecost.

490/8-9. *I haffe desyredde...*: Luc. 22: 5.

492/22. *venye*: The venia is a gesture of humility, a complete prostration upon the ground. It is described as a Dominican devotion in Clark's translation of Suso's *Life of the Servant*, p. 27, n. 1. On 507/11 of these revelations "prostrate lyenge-downe" refers to the venia.

498/17. *meke ande lawelye subieccion*: These injunctions to pursue perfect obedience are repeated several times: e.g., 503/21-504/2, 505/20-506/2.

502/7. *Adherens...*: Cf. 1 Cor. 6: 17.

504/16-507/14. This chapter includes some details of the rite of profession, notably the acceptance of the yoke of the Rule, the singing of the litany, and the Communion of the newly professed. St. Gertrude's fourth exercise, called Renewal of Monastic Profession, alludes to these ceremonies (*Exercises*, pp. 53-78).

504/21-22. *I schalle goo...*: 2 Cor. 6: 16.

507/12. *pennancz ande repentaunce ande ... satysfaccioun*: These (contrition, penance, and satisfaction) are the constituent parts of the sacrament of penance.

509/15-510/8. This chapter is an example of patchwork extraction in the shorter *Liber*. S includes the angel's explanation of his "knowing" and also describes the elaborate spectacle of the angel's offering to God. See *Revelationes*, 2: 279. *Lownessee* 510/8 translates "clemencie."

509/16. *in the cloystre*: The usual practice in Benedictine monasteries was to recite the Office of Prime partly in the cloister and partly in the choir; in succeeding ages some monasteries performed the whole Office, together with the Martyrology in the choir (Dolan, *St. Gertrude the Great*, p. 125 n.). Perhaps the "grete necessyte" (509/15) refers to the period when the interdict was imposed on Helfta.

512/8. *Benedictus...*: Cf. Dan. 3: 56.

514/12. *Respice...*: This appears to be an adaptation of the Solemn Collects recited on Good Friday.

515/2. *Emitte...*: Responsory of the Sundays of August.

515/8-9. *O wonderfulle luffe ... ande wonderfulle prys*: This translates C's "O mira dilectio circa nos et O admirabile precium" which are adaptations of the first words of two separate prayers from the liturgy of Holy Week.

516/3. *two eeres*: King, *Liturgy of the Roman Church*, p. 107, mentions that ministerial chalices of the early Middle Ages were often provided with handles to facilitate the administration of the Sacrament.

517/3-7. *Botte whene ... be to hym*: The *Booke* omits part of C's reading: "sed cum homo grauamen suum ipse vult portare labitur in impacienciam et quo plus tractat nunc inde loquendo nunc cogitando eo grauius et amarius inde affligitur."

521/10. *playe with my luffynge dowȝttere*: God playing with man is compared to a mother playing with her child in *The Chastising of God's Children*, p. 98/4 and note, p. 263.

523/1. *In...*: Cf. Ezech. 18: 22.

524/8. *he takes itt for a grete ande a cherelye gyfte*: C has "pro magno et caro habebit." B's variant reading "clere" indicates that both scribes had difficulty in deciphering the word in the parent copy. The original ME was probably "dere."

525/1. *of here vnkyndenesse*: This translates C's "ingratitudine"; S reads "in gratitudine."

537/17-18. *v thowsande*: Woolf, *English Religious Lyric*, p. 204, remarks that the arithmetical calculation referred to occurred often in poems on the Passion and that the cult was "designed to bring the saying of the paternoster (the standard lay devotion) into relation with the Passion." E's marginal gloss "Nota bene" calls attention to the entire chapter. See Note 178/10-11.

538/7. *importunite*: It is possible that the scribe intended to cancel this word and retain "importune" which follows. The latter had great currency as an adjective in the fifteenth century, and "importunite" was used as a noun in the same period. "Importunate" (adj.) was used in the first half of the sixteenth century; possibly E's word is a variant.

539/2-9. *Itte suffice ... both lyve ande dede*: This direction is the translator's addition.

542/4-5. *whome folowes ... clepynge agayne*: C reads "quem tanta subsequitur clemencia paterne reuocacionis."

542/10-552/3. The letters which comprise the next four chapters are said to be copies of Mechtild's own compositions (*Revelationes*, 2: 310, n. 1). The first three were sent to the same person, evidently a young nun. Dom Jean Leclercq, "Le genre épistolaire au moyen âge," *Revue du moyen âge latin*, 2 (April, 1946), 63-70 has surveyed the principal types within the genre of monastic letters as codified in the "artes dictandi." Letters of dedication, exhortation, recommendation, and doctrinal consultation are some of the representative forms. Mechtild's correspondence can be classified as spiritual direction, wherein edifying thoughts provide the inspiration. There is some attention paid to rhetorical structure and language, particularly in the elaborate scheme of the first letter and in the extended similitude of the second.

547/13-16. *Ande ryght als a kynge ... emange his frendys*: This is an attempt to render C's erroneous "Sicut rex qui sponsam suam mundam perduxit in domum suam urbem aut ciuitatem aliquam diuicijs plenam amicis suis in pignus exponit." S has "nondum" where C has "mundam."

552/12. *Symon...*: Joann. 21: 15, 16.

557/7. *Misericordia...*: Psal. 88: 15.

558/5. *here foundere*: Burchard, count of Mansfeld; see above, p. 33.

558/19. *two abbesses*: Cunegunde von Halberstadt (d. 1251) and Gertrude von Hackeborn (d. 1291).

560/9. *erle*: This appears to be a mistake. The founder, Burchard, died shortly after establishing the monastery in 1229. In the Solesmes text, the "erle" is referred to as Count Burchard and is identified by the editor as the descendant of the founder. This later Burchard died in 1294. See *Revelationes*, 2: 336. Cf. 563/21.

567/8-12. *Offe ... mysvnderestode*: This passage does not appear in any of the Latin versions examined; it appears to be the interpolation of the translator.

568/12. *chapelle*: This refers to the chapel at Helfta founded by the son of the founder in 1265, where some of the nobles of the Mansfeld family were buried; see *Revelationes*, 2: 336, 341, notes.

570/2. *whare the sowlys were...*: This question appears to have intrigued the medieval mind. Tauler, in one of his sermons cautioning against "high speculations" alludes to the uncertainty of salvation for Solomon and Origen (quoted in Ancelet-Hustache's *Master Eckhart*, p. 152). The Solesmes editor notes (*Revelationes*, 2: 344) that the St. Gall manuscript has a marginal comment after this passage; it reads: "Quid autem bonitas mea cum Aristotelis anima fecerit, volo celare, ne philosophus naturalis coelestia et supernaturalia minus curet."

572/1, 5. *sauoures*; *sauourynge*: These words follow C's "fragrat," "fragrans." S has "flagrat," "flagrans."

572/18. *dirige*: This is the first word of the antiphon from the Office of the Dead and is used as a name for that service. C has "vigilias."

573/2. *Si que illis...*: Versicle from the former Office of the Dead. (*Revelationes*, 2: 346 n.)

573/5-16. *lettynge*: This is followed in both the complete and abridged versions of the *Liber* by an explanation of the symbolic meaning of the forefeet.

575/5. *Fons Viuus...*: C reads: "Legite oracionem illam que dicitur Fons Viuus, Beati immaculati cum oracione sibi asscripta et magnum adiutorium inde sencient et iuuamen."

575/5. *Beati...*: Psal. 118.

575/6. *Ad ... tribularer*: beginning of Psal. 119.

575/6. *domine ... me*: beginning of Psal. 138.

575/18-19. *Ande howe ... prayere*: See Note 60/16-17.

576/7. *Pater Noster qui es...*: Fr. Thurston ("The *Our Father* in English," *Familiar Prayers*, pp. 22-37) surveys the early extant versions of the prayer in the vernacular and draws these conclusions: that down to the time of the

Reformation the only official form was the Latin; that early English trans-
lations evidence divergences in text; and that the now familiar authorized
version was introduced in 1539. The Exposition of the Pater was a familiar
formula in medieval instruction; see *The Book of Vices and Virtues*, ed. W. N.
Francis (EETS 217, 1942), pp. 98, and 333-9 for some examples.

583/2. *grummelynge*: The only fifteenth-century citations in MED are
"grummede" and "grummynge" based on MDu. "grommen." The *Booke*'s
word appears to be influenced by Fr. "grommelen." Earliest example in OED
of "to grumble" is 1586.

584/19. *Erit...*: Cf. 1 Cor. 15: 28.

585/18. *two mennys*: This refers to the original compilers at Helfta (cf. *two
persones* 587/17 and 592/5) who are thought to be St. Gertrude and another
nun (*Revelationes*, 2: 355, n. 1). The male writer referred to in chs. 16 and
22 below is also a misunderstanding.

586/3-4. *allebeitt þowe haffes fulfyllede me*: A long section omitted
describes the experience and illumination referred to. This chapter, up to
587/15, is a melange of disconnected bits extracted from Part 1, ch. 22 of the
longer *Liber*. See *Revelationes*, 2: 353-5.

589/13. *namenede*: This might be scribal error for the more common
"nemen—" (ME "nemn") 58/3, 556/5, 557/15, 19 or confusion with
"name" (OE "namian").

590/1. *Domine...*: Matt. 25: 20.

593/12. *Benedicta...*: Introit, Mass of Trinity Sunday.

593/21. *iiij vertues*: Five virtues are listed in ch. 18.

596/3-599/10. The material comprising these three chapters (19, 20, 21)
is printed in the Solesmes edition but Dom Paquelin indicates that it did not
appear in his basic text, the Guelferbytanus manuscript. He copied it from a
sixteenth-century Latin version (*Revelationes*, 2: xii, 361).

596/9. *Redemptor...*: Responsory, 1 Lesson.

598/12. *Stabat...*: Joann. 19: 25.

599/10. *receyvere of persones*: C has "personarum acceptor." The phrase
is rendered "acceptour of persones" in other ME writings and is listed under
that wording in the MED. It means one who shows partiality.

600/18-21. *Ande foralsmoche as lytelle ... þis worschepfulle persone*: C
has "Sed quia ipsius uenerande persone uitam et conuersacionem laudabilem
et uere imitabilem [S: 'mirabilem'] minus descripsimus...."

601/9. *werye*: This adj. is based on "ware" (variant "were") and is not
recorded before 1552. See OED "ware," "wary" adj. C has "cauebat."

603/9. *þare was nevere oone...*: This statement is interpreted as a modest
disclaimer by the author, St. Gertrude. At this time her own fame far
outstripped Mechtild's (*Revelationes*, 2: 365).

604/1. *so many orysons ande prayers*: This activity of Mechtild insures her place in devotional manuals; see above p. 46, n. 50.

604/8. *before lentyne*: Henry Suso also lamented the riotous celebrations on Shrove Tuesday; *Life of the Servant*, pp. 38-40.

607/3-21. *Also sche ... fayre wordes*: This is taken piecemeal from the long first chapter of Part 6 of the fuller *Liber* (*Revelationes*, 2: 373-7), which describes the virtues of Abbess Gertrude.

607/4. *a grete herte*: Possibly "herte" is a corruption of "heede" (heed). C reads "De infirmis maxima illi erat cura...."

607/19-20. *þame þat were vndere here*: Preger, *Geschichte*, 1: 81, in noting the interpolated material in this chapter (see Note 607/3-21), points out the inappropriateness of speaking of subordinates who were supposed to have been inspired by Mechtild's example. Nowhere else is Mechtild said to have held an office which would have her assign other nuns to do lowly work.

610/3. *brynnynge brande*: Eccli. 48: 1.

610/4-611/4. *Tharefore sche ... tawȝt or redde*: This section is also a collection of fragments from Part 6, ch. 1 of the complete *Liber*; see Note 607/3-21.

611/11-12. *in whos dayes nowe es comme þe ende of þe werlde*: The same observation is made in the prologue; cf. 66/11-12 and Note.

611/12-13. *þe fylthes or drawȝtes of alle vycis*: C has "feces omnium viciorum." Manuscript B's "draftes" is a recorded variant (MED "draf" n.). The word is often used figuratively for moral filth or corruption. E's "drawȝtes" might be a scribal alteration of "drafts" but it is also possible that it might be pl. ME "draught" in the sense of a figurative association with entrails (MED "draught" n., 5c).

611/15. *Gregour ... Ezechielle*: Gregory the Great preached 22 sermons on Ezechiel to the people of Rome in 593-4.

611/20. *Danyel*: (Dan. 12: 4) Gregory's *Homilarium in Ezechielem*, 2.4, *P.L.* 76, col. 979.

612/5. *Dauid*: (Psal. 118: 100) Gregory's *Moralium*, 11.15, *P.L.* 75, col. 965.

Select Glossary

In general, this glossary aims at explaining unfamiliar forms and words. Some commonplace words are included and some words are more fully glossed to show any or all of the following: senses not current today, varying forms of possible linguistic interest, occurrences in set phrases, unusual grammatical functions.

References given are limited, not a full record. No distinction in the references is made between spellings of a word containing (1) both single and double vowel symbols (e.g., *freelte, frelte*) or (2) a suffix in *-ion/-ioun* or *-ante/-aunte*. Verbs are ordinarily entered under their infinitive form.

Within an entry, the sign ~ represents any of the forms of the head-word. Among the abbreviations, *pr.p.* and *pp.* stand for present participle and past participle respectively. Page and line numbers are usually the first occurrence of the word or sense. A line number repeated indicates two appearances of the word in the line. An asterisk denotes an emended form.

In the alphabetical order, ʒ follows *g*, and *þ* is placed as an alternative to *th*. When *y* represents a vowel it is treated as a variant of *i*, and consonantal *i* is treated as *j*. Vocalic and consonantal *u* and *v* have separate places under *u* and *v*.

aane see **o, oo**.

aanlye, anelye *adv*. only 422/15, 471/19.

abbytte see **habyte**.

abyde *v*. await, continue, remain (no *prep.*) 485/12, 497/20; **abayde** *pa.t. sg. & pl.* 81/9, 83/9, 86/6; **aboyde** 97/16 ([he] missing), 200/16; **abydene** *pp.* 380/9.

able *adj*. likely 466/17, 548/12.

able *v*. adapt, prepare 385/16; **habbils** *pr. 3 sg.* 318/10; **abellede** *pp.* 464/22.

abowne *adv*. above 29/4, 189/1; **abovene** 6/13.

abreggynge *vbl. n.* relieving 394/4.

abrode *adv*. widely apart 81/16, 606/2; **obrede** 201/4.

absorte *pp.* (*aux.* missing) absorbed 602/23.

accepte *adj*. acceptable 40/11, 430/11.

acceptede *adj*. agreeable, pleasing 481/14, 491/15.

accesse *n*. approaching 458/10.

acounte (*for*) *v*. consider, hold to be 435/13; **acomptede** *pp.* 118/20; **acowntede** esteemed 438/12.

acownte *n.*; *to* ~ of worth 563/10.

addamant, ademaunde *n*. a hard gem *355/4, 10.

addylle, adelle *v*. earn 501/4, 6.

affliccions *n. pl.* mortifications 64/3.

agayne *prep*. in front of 89/8; near, towards 338/15; contrary to 374/8.

agaynes *prep*. opposed to 69/12; **agayns** in the sight of 523/8; with respect to 172/3; in front of 133/22; **ageyns** 397/2; ~ *hym* not in his best interest 525/20.

ayenste *prep*. near 9/1; **aʒens** 265/9; **aʒenste** against 441/1.

ayredde *pr. 1 sg.* reckon 195/1.

aythere *adj.*; ~ *oþere* each other 266/14-15.

alange *adv.*; *alle* ~ from end to end 78/9.

alle *adv.* completely 5/21; ~*anlye* only 340/11; ~*ouere* in every part 162/5; ~ *ʒiffe* even though 430/11, 438/19; *for* ~ 452/6-7.

Alle Hallues *n. pl.* All Saints 271/7.

almarye, almerye *n.* repository 549/1, 548/17.

almesse *n.* alms 538/7; **almesses** *pl.* good deeds 564/17.

almessemane *n.* bedesman 538/6.

almuse *n.* alms 527/5; **allmus** 565/6.

alonelye *adj.* alone, only 603/18.

also(o) *adv.* as 146/18, 539/13.

amende *v.* give satisfaction for 161/16, 186/6; *refl.* reform 507/13; **amendede** *of pp.* converted from 326/3.

ammonycioun *n.* reproof 330/16.

ane-corde *n.* agreement 470/23.

anye *adj.* any 40/5; **eny** 425/18; **ony** 610/17.

appayraylede *pa.t. sg. embellished* 323/19; *pp.* 277/15.

ar see **or.**

arawe *adv.* one after another 128/19.

areche *v.* reach in thought 393/16.

arere *v.* exalt 363/20.

articulle, artycle, artykelle, artykille *n.* component part 409/20, 410/17, 411/3, 11.

aseth *n.*; *make* ~ make atonement 79/10, 172/3.

askes *n. pl.* ashes 74/20, 75/19.

aspyes *n. pl.* snares 302/1.

associate *pp.* joined 611/7.

associede (*to*) *pp.* associated (with) 608/18.

assoyle *v.* absolve 271/16.

atte *conj.* that 106/11.

atte *prep.* at the 304/10; in 467/10.

atteyne *v.* understand 98/12.

auntere, awntere *n.*; *in* ~in case, lest 75/11, 120/21, 239/6.

autere, awtere *n.* altar 4/10, 6/20, 342/10, 19.

avaywnsede *pp.* moved forward 524/17.

auysely *adv.* attentively 442/22.

avysemente *n.* deliberation, reflection 168/5, 288/17; resolution 507/8.

awe *pr. 1 & 3 sg.* ought 75/11, 115/1.

baldelye *adv.* confidently 534/3; **boldelye** 171/11.

bawme *n.* balsam 177/7.

be *v.* be 14/23, 360/4, 364/2; (no *prep.* 521/6); **bene** 346/21; **ham** *pr. 1 sg.* 203/7; **erte** *2 sg.* 82/11, 166/15, 16; **es** *3 sg.* 1/3, 4/21 etc.; **ys** 50/19, 66/21 etc.; **ere** *pl.* 116/3, 575/7; **beys** *imp. pl.* 113/3, 5, 7; **ware** *pa.t. pl.* 5/8, 72/15, 158/22; **warre** 121/14, 358/19; **was** 203/13, 394/2, 407/11, 582/16; **were** *subj. sg.* might be 53/11, 432/16.

beclippe *v.* embrace, clasp 16/14; **beclep-pyde** *pa.t. sg.* 28/13; **becleppede** *pp.* encircled 93/20.

becomen *pr. 3 pl.* befall 66/11.

before or *conj.* previous to the time when 589/18.

behalde *v.* observe, look at 109/3, 126/19; (no *prep.*) 39/11; **beholde** examine 12/8; **behelde** *pa.t. pl.* observed 17/12, 107/5.

beheestis *n. pl.* promises 39/8, 417/11.

behete *pr. subj. sg.* promise 507/13, 567/1; **behette** *pa.t. 1 sg.* 533/11.

belewe *n.* bellows 427/7.

beneme *pr. subj. sg.* take away *65/3.

bent(e) *n.* necklace *173/10; chain 548/8.

berdene *n.* child in the womb 81/21; load, cares 197/15; **bordene** 514/10; **burdyne** 331/6.

berye *v.* bury *31/5, 363/12, 18; **byrrye** 167/1; **bere** 174/18.

berynges *vbl. n. pl.* gestures 76/16.

besauntes *n. pl.* coins 590/3.

besemys *pr. 3 sg.*; *itt* ~ *hym noʒt* it is not befitting to him 517/8-9.

besye *adj.* constant 45/16; earnest 86/11, 14; diligent 170/13; ~ *to* devoted to 452/12.

besynes *n.* solicitude 610/5, activity, work 8/13, 149/21; **bysynes** 19/23; *do þy* ~ take pains 186/6.

betynge *adj.* biting 442/16.

betternesse *n.* anguish 74/18; **bitternesse** 350/22; *pl.* 103/13.

bydde *pr. 1 sg.* invite 88/1; **bad(d)e** *pa.t. 3 sg.* prayed 20/2; commanded, enjoined 1/22, 9/5; **boode** *pp.* 250/3; **bodene** 276/9.

blyssehede *n.* blessedness 293/4.

blode *n.* blood 40/1, 179/2, 21; **bloyde** 116/6, 224/4; **on-bloyde** bloody 604/17.

bochere *n.* butcher 443/7.

bodene, boode see **bydde.**

boystowse *adj.* loud 525/21.

borowh *n.* surety 171/11.

bowe *v.* incline, bend down 209/9; **bowe** *pr. subj. sg.* influence 193/2; ~ *his herte* bend in submission 472/3; *refl.* submit 112/8; **bowede** *downe his eeres pa.t. sg.* turned his attention to 424/12; **bowede** *pp.* curved, bent 158/2, 13.

bowynge *adj.* submissive 492/15.

box(e) *n.* pyx 140/10, 11, 254/14; **boksys** *pl.* boxes 124/1.

breye *pr. 3 pl.* howl 467/10.

brenne *v.* burn (*inf.* for *pr.p.*) 16/19, 235/7; **brennande** *pr. p.* 335/20, 371/4; **brende** *pp.* 236/5; **brente** 124/6; **for-brente** burnt up 574/16.

breste *pr. subj. sg.* be overwhelmed 346/6; **braste** *oute pa.t. sg. & pl.* burst forth 243/13; **brostene** *pp.* broken 382/5; **brostene** *owte* torn open 496/14; **brostyne** shattered 355/10.

bryght *adv.* brightly 29/20, 351/19.

broche *n.* jeweled ornament, necklace 227/15, 246/19.

can *pr. 1 sg.* know 563/3; **cane** am able to 67/2; **kan** *pl.* 529/15; **kunne** 330/15; **cowth(e)** *pa.t. sg.* could 24/12, 29/18 etc.; **kowde** 350/19; **kowth** 287/5.

cene *n.*; *laste* ~ Last Supper *109/6.

chaarge *v.*; *es to* ~ is of importance 498/1; **charechynge** *pr. p.*; *noght* ~ *itt* making no account of it 425/6; **chargede** *pp.* burdened 331/4.

chalengede *pa.t. pl.* accused 169/4; **chalanchede** *pp.* claimed 559/17.

chastede *pa.t. sg.* disciplined 425/11.

chastynges *n. pl.* chastenings 604/7.

chawffede *adj.* inflamed 89/10.

cheyne *n.* chain 184/5, 7, 11; **chyne** 304/19, 305/4.

cherede *adj.*; *gladde* ~ cheerful 610/14-15.

chese *v.* choose 382/16, 17; **cheese** *pa.t. sg.* 595/5; **chesydde** 171/9; **chase** 247/4, 6; **choyse** *pp.* 547/22.

chesynge *vbl. n.* election 290/4.

choris *n. pl.* dances 275/5.

circumcide *pr. subj. sg.* circumcise 111/4, 113/2; **circumcied** 4/18.

claryficacion *n.* glorification 191/15.

cledde see **clowth.**

clepe *v.* call 77/14, 88/5.

clerelye *adv.* entirely, purely 562/15.

clerenesse *n.* completeness 313/16; splendour, brightness 38/19; **cleernys** 242/12.

clyppyynges *vbl. n.* embracings 488/15.

cloystere *n.* enclosure 192/20.

cloyth *v.* clothe 521/16; **cledde** *pa.t. pl.* 144/20; **clowthede** *pp.* 153/9.

cloth *n.* garment 4/23; **cloyth** 175/13.

clowtede *pp.* patched 602/14.

clowtes *n. pl.* rags 602/12.

cold(e) *adj.* withdrawn (from) *36/19, 399/3, 20.

colecte *n.* prayer during Mass 104/8; **colett** 3/14.

come *v.* come 1/9, (no *prep.*) 485/13; **commys** *pr. 3 sg.* becomes 378/15. Phr. ~ *to* (*oneself*) recover consciousness 606/5; recover from distraction or spiritual absorption 517/7, 603/6-7.

comerede, **commerede** *pp.* encumbered, held fast 597/9, 13.

comfortable *adj.* strengthening, encouraging 410/6-7, 540/7.

comfortatyfe *adj.* sustaining 95/12.

commynge *vbl. n.* excessive visiting 72/22.

commodyte *n.* convenience 217/10.

commune *v.* share *419/19; **comowne** 206/21; **commwnede** *pa.t. 3 sg.* administered the Holy Communion 18/2; **communede** *pp.* associated *611/7; **comonyd** communicated 6/2.

competente *adj.* suitable 338/15.

comprehendyd *pp.* encompassed 390/3.

conceyle *pr. 1 sg.* advise 532/16; **counseyle** *3 sg.* 116/4.

conceyte *n.* opinion 146/16.

conceyue *pr. 1 sg.* take in 157/11; **conceyuede** *pp.* comprised 101/18.

condicion *n.* disposition 340/10.

connynge *n.* ability 67/10; **cunnynge** wisdom, knowledge, 612/16; **kunnynge** 73/7, 226/22.

conuenable *adj.* suitable 100/6, 432/17.

conuersacion *n.* mode of life 41/13, 42/1 etc.; former life 439/14.

corneers *n. pl.* points 246/19.

cors *n.* body 374/3.

countenaunce *n.* demeanour 94/16; **cowntenaunz** gesture 388/7; **cowntenaunces** *pl.* 606/1.

couple *n.* bond 197/12.

course *n.* turn 138/22.

coule *n.* tub 331/3.
cowrse *n.* curse 132/6.
crache *n.* manger 99/2, 102/1.
craftye *adj.* skillful 277/17.
creature *n.*[1] creation 179/18; person 9/10, 67/15, 222/18.
creature *n.*[2] creator 77/16.
culuere *n.* dove 41/21, 81/16.
cure *n.* care 462/10.
curiosite *n.* inquisitive learning 456/8.
curiouse *adj.* intricate, abstruse *612/15; **curyous(e)** exquisite 484/7; skillful, elaborate 82/18.
customeablye *adv.* customarily *119/18.

daynte *adj.* dear, precious 351/16.
dawynge *n.* dawn 150/18.
dede *n.* death 58/21, 59/2; **deyde** 103/2, 151/21; **deth** 14/9, 155/9; *the ~* 151/18, 172/7.
defawte *n.* defect, fault 142/10, 157/12; failure of duty 169/4; *for ~ of* in the absence of 490/13; **defawȝttes** *pl.* misdeeds 494/1.
defawtye *adj.* defective 503/4.
defowledde, defowlede *pa.t. pl.* defiled 398/9; *pp.* disfigured 300/20.
degre *n.* state 133/8; **degrees** *pl.* ranks 78/9; stages, levels 142/7.
dey *v.* die 70/18; **dye** 209/19, 210/1.
delefullye *adv.* mournfully 380/6.
delese *pr. 3 sg.* distributes 527/5; **deyleys** 283/2.
delfynge *vbl. n.* digging 330/11.
delycate *adj.* delightful 241/8; exquisitely fine 247/16, 550/16.
delycatelye *adv.* indulgently 425/13.
delice *n.* delight 572/8.
delycious *adj.* highly pleasing 29/23, 77/7.
delyciousite *n.* delight *107/13.
demynge *vbl. n.* judgment 113/7, 114/1.
departynge *vbl. n.* separation 166/22; division 534/19.
depressyoune *n.* humility 493/3.
dereworth *adj.* costly 91/3.
derkenesse *n.* secrecy 360/4; evil 239/5.
desyre *n.* petition 222/1, 307/23; (with *to, for*) yearning for 17/2, 140/18.
desyres *pr. 3 sg.* longs for 245/2; (with *aftere, to* & *obj.*) 220/6-7, 300/9; **desyrede** *pa.t. sg.* requested 53/6, 7.
desyrows *adj.* desirable 533/13.
despyte *n.* contempt 45/14; insult 161/11, 16; *hadde in ~, dyspyte* scorned 83/23, 470/6.
despitowse *adj.* pitiless 463/20.
desponsacion *n.* espousal 409/10, 15.
deuere *n.* duty 432/3.
dewels *n. pl.* devils 159/7.
dignacioun *n.* gracious condescension 133/9.
dignyte *n.* company 396/16. See Note 122/10.
dirige *n.* matins in office of the dead 572/18.
dysciplyne *n.* instruction 298/5; **disciplynes** *pl.* penitential mortification 34/3.
dyscomforthede *adj.* disheartened 72/18.
discres *n.* decrease 431/9.
diseses *pr. 3 sg.* troubles 372/23.
dyspysene *pr. pl.* defy 161/15; **dyspysede** *pa.t. sg.* disregarded 493/19.
dyspytouslye *adv.* cruelly 162/19, 172/16.
dyspoyses *pr. 3 sg.* arranges 204/17; **dyspoysede** *pa.t. sg. refl.* prepared himself 576/16.
dyuerses *adj.* perverse 349/7.
do *v.* carry out, do perform; **dede** *pa.t. 1 & 3 sg.* 11/14, 14/4, 372/16; **dyede** 284/3, 355/23. Phr. *~ after* act in compliance with 49/18; *~ awaye* efface, abolish 172/8, 223/10 etc.; *~the to witte* inform you 587/14.
doyenge *vbl. n.* conduct 261/4.
dome *n.* judgment 10/12, 88/5.
dowte *n.* doubt 24/5, 94/1; **dowȝtes** *pl.* fears 29/10.
drawe *v.* draw, lead 1/10; **drawht** 464/3; *imp. sg.* 463/18; **droght** *pa.t. sg.* 336/11, 337/7; **drow(e)** 26/17, 78/10 ([she] missing) 1/11, 74/10; **drowht** 420/11; **drewe** took 30/1, 19; **drawene** *pp.* stretched 264/6; lifted 458/15.
drawȝt *n.* drawing 548/11.
drawȝtes *n. pl.* dregs 611/12.
drawynge *vbl. n.*; *~ instrumente* bucket 282/17, 22.
drede *v.*; *es to ~is* to be feared 603/10.
dredefulle *adj.* fearful, timid 28/19, 215/15; **dredfulle** formidable 375/20.
dreght see **drye**.
drye *adj.* withered 153/13; hard, cold 540/20; barren, unfruitful 153/17; **dreght** 528/11.
droght see **drawe**.
droppede *pa.t. sg.* dripped, trickled 145/5, 590/16.
droppys *n. pl.* jewel droplets 139/19.

ductour *n.* guide 198/6.

dulnes(se) *n.* lack of ardour 465/16; stupidity 533/20.

dwelle *v.* abide, remain 8/1, 142/5; **twelle** 13/7.

eche *adj.* each; ~*a* every 308/1.

eeyen(e) *n. pl.* eyes 233/20, 21; **eeyne** 477/5; **yn** 380/14.

eernese *n.* pledge 227/11.

effectualle *adj.* profound 2/16; **effectuele** 93/9, 19.

effectuallye *adv.* zealously 243/12.

effectueslye *adv.* earnestly 165/3; **effectu-ouslye** really 81/22.

eftesones *adv.* again 141/7.

egyr *adj.* biting, sharp 422/19.

eyre *n.* heir 396/14; **eyres** *pl.* 291/20; **heyres** 190/7.

elacyone *n.* vainglory 494/6.

elde *n.* age 341/12.

eldere *adj. comp.* older 220/1; ~ *aage* adolescence 277/4; ~*men* men of ancient times 612/7.

embrowdede *pp.* embroidered 566/10; **en-broudede** 203/15; **enbrowdede** 326/23.

empte *n.* ant 586/9.

enfourme *v.* instruct 472/7; **informeth** *pr. 3 sg.* inspires 591/13.

enhause, enhawse *v.* exalt, praise 195/14, 400/15; **enhauncede** *pp.* 311/16.

enpeyres *pr. 3 sg.* damages, corrupts 43/18.

ensample *n.* an illustrative instance 379/4; **insampulle** 33/16; *in, to* **ensaumple** as an example 307/21, 312/14-15.

enserchede, inserchede *pp.* searched into; *maye noght (now3t) be* ~ cannot be comprehended 323/18, 415/12, 462/8-9.

entende *pr. subj. sg.* devote attention 400/18.

ententyfe *adj.* assiduous, heedful 400/16.

erbeys *n. pl.* herbs 150/3; **erbes** 151/7.

euen(e) *adj.* fellow 85/21, 113/14, 136/4; ~ *to* level with 339/12.

even(e) *adv.*; ~*streyght* directly, immediately 573/15; ~*vpperyght* straight up 438/15.

euere *adj.* every 9/18, 288/2.

euere(ye) *n.* ivory 92/15, 317/10, 363/9; **euerye** 31/2, 92/8, 363/17.

eueryeche *adj.* every 311/20.

excercyse *n.* practice, spiritual training 34/22, 72/6, 237/7; **excercise** service *474/13.

excercitacion *n.* devotional exercise 170/17.

expenses *n. pl.* payments 443/17; *made ...* **exspensis** made outlays of money, gave donations 564/12.

fayle, faylle *v.* come to an end 111/17; languish 235/5; lack, want, fall short of 213/17; **falleys** *pr. 3 sg.* 213/20; **fayll-ede** *pa.t. 3 sg.* diminished 229/21.

falle *v.* befall, happen 545/5; **falleth** *pr. sg. impers.* is fitting 516/14; **falle** *subj.* sin 75/14; **felle** *pa.t. 3 sg.* succumbed 516/23. *Phr.* ~ *in thoughtys* became troubled 153/3; ~ *into no3t fro hereselfe* ? was transported 75/18-19, see Note; ~ *into syekenesse* became ill 57/18; ~ *to (here) mynde, sawle* occurred to (her) 150/10.

farys *pr. 3 sg.* appears 145/8.

fastyne *v.* imprint 156/12; **fastne** *pr. 1 sg.* 223/21; **festyne** attach, fasten 174/21; **festonede** *pp.* inflicted 530/11.

fauour *imp. sg.* incline to 187/2.

fawte *n.* fault 8/5.

fedynge *adj.* nourishing; *fulle* ~ completely filling 200/8.

fedynge *vbl. n.* rich food 364/1; nourishment 472/15.

feerslye *adv.* rapidly 436/13; **ferselye** forcefully 145/4.

feersnes *n.* force, intensity 257/13; **feyrse-nesse** 544/2; **fersenesse** 102/18; **ferese-nes** eagerness 331/2; **fersnes** ferocity 103/6.

feyghttys *pr. 3 sg.* fights, struggles 209/1; *pl.* 267/2.

felaschippe *n.* company 127/12; **felaw-scheppe** companionship 181/22.

felawlye *adv.* sociably 297/24; **felowlye** familiarly, on equal terms 233/14; **folow-ly** 259/7.

felawschepe *pa.t. 3 sg.* united in fellowship, associated 190/5.

felynge *vbl. n.* awareness, consciousness 77/9, 107/1, 3, 4 etc.; understanding 98/11, 101/2.

fellye *adv.* cruelly 165/3.

ferre *adv.* far 42/23; by far 319/10.

feruente *adj.* hot 220/2.

fylth(e) *n.* sin, corruption 215/21, 280/22; stain 592/14; **felthe** 310/20.

fynde *v.* find, discover 30/21; *(refl.)* come to be 581/19; **fyndeth** *pr. 3 sg. (refl.)* perceives 423/16; **fyende** *subj.* obtain

420/3; **fande** *pa.t. 3 sg. & pl.* found 33/8, 99/1, 150/14.

fyre *adj.* flaming with fire 26/14, 335/15.

fle *pr. 3 sg.* flies 439/11; **flees** ([it] missing) 484/1; **fleys** 107/14; **flow(e)** *pa.t. 3 sg. & pl.* 9/20, 158/4.

flee *v.* escape 529/16; **fleys** *pr. 3 sg.* flys for help 196/22.

floode *n.* river, stream 178/17, 329/10, 17.

floryschynge (*oute*) *pr. p.* shooting forth 270/6; **florischede** *pa.t. sg.* abounded (in) 327/9; **floreschede** blossomed, flourished 120/14; **floryschede** (*pp.* for *inf.*) 372/3.

folowande *adj.* that now follow(s) 594/8; **folowynge** 66/6.

foralsmekille, foralsmekylle *adv.* inasmuch 10/10, 351/9.

forbere *v.* hold back 133/15; (*refl.*) refrain 54/8; *pr. subj. sg.* submit to 486/15.

forne-choyse *adj.* pre-elected 548/2.

fors *refl. imp. sg.* strive 445/3.

for-spetede *pp.*; *alle* ~ spat upon all over 161/11.

for-woundede *pp.* cut all over 604/16.

fowle *adj.* disgracefully 43/15, 455/16.

fre(e) *adj.* generous, liberal 250/14, 287/11; not in bondage to sin 61/12, 109/20.

frelte *n.* frailty, moral weakness 75/14, 517/1.

freteth *pr. 3 sg.* gnaws 573/12; **fretynge** *pr. p.* 573/8.

from *prep.*; ~ *hereselfe* out of her wits 338/10.

fruycion *n.* pleasurable possession 596/1.

fulfyllynge *vbl. n.* filling, completion 76/12; compensation 560/20, 577/2.

furth(e) *adv.*; *so* ~ then in regular order 19/14; similarly 129/20; ~ *with* along with them 78/16.

gastefulnesse *n.* terror 120/19.

gastelye *adv.* in spirit, spiritually 39/11, 156/18.

geant *n.* giant 90/23.

gentele *adj.* well-born 108/19; see **smalle**.

gerdede *pp.* invested 75/2.

gete *v.* get, acquire 23/4; **gate, gatte** *pa.t. 1 sg.* obtained 373/10, 410/14; *3 sg.* 401/17; **gettyne** *pp.* received 72/8.

gettene *adj.* begotten 393/12.

gyeve *v.* give 25/4, 66/1, 76/8; **gyffe** 50/3, 82/14. Phr. ~ *a flyght* fly 246/5; ~

(*oneself*) exert (oneself) 390/1; ~ *a sangge* sing 181/13-14.

gyfte *n.* gift 31/18; *geftes of nature* natural endowments 73/6.

gloryouste *n.* resplendence 173/9.

glosynge *vbl. n.* coaxing 71/22.

gobet(te) *n.* lump, mass 202/10, 266/1, 467/6; fragment 590/10, 11.

god(e) *adj.* good 47/12, 191/10, 511/12, 15; **gude** 327/10, 342/6.

goddenesse *n.* benevolence 429/18; **gudnesse** 341/5.

gone *v.* go, walk 91/12; **gane** *pp.* 339/2. Phr. ~ **a processioun** walk in procession 15/14-15, 18/8.

gouernere *n.* tutor 80/8.

gracyous *adj.* endowed with divine grace *73/14, 311/4.

grauntede, graunttede *here pa.t. 3 sg.* agreed to her request 25/9-10, 301/8.

grauynge, gravynge *vbl. n.* carving, sculpture 277/17, 22.

grees *n.* step in a flight 19/14, 143/6, 7, 8, 11, 12; *pl.* 8/2, 19/13; **greses** 265/4.

grenes(se) *n.* greenness, freshness 153/15, 236/17, 258/17.

grennede *pa.t. pl.*; ~... *with here teth* snarled in anger 373/9-10.

grete *pa.t. 3 sg.* made great 81/20.

grewyne *pp.*; *oolde* ~ become settled 69/22.

gruchynge *vbl. n.* complaining, murmuring 73/18, 170/15; **grutchynges** *pl.* 424/14.

grummelynge *pr.p.* muttering 583/2. See Note.

ȝaa *adv.* yes 599/9.

ȝaat(e) *n.* door 184/3, 6, 9, 10.

ȝalowe *adj.* golden 286/21.

ȝe *pron. nom. 2 pl.* you 65/17, 67/12, 16, 68/6, 83/23; **ȝowe** 412/1, 444/7; **ye** 67/17, 68/5; **ȝowe** *dat.* 115/20, 182/1; **yowe** *acc. & dat.* 66/3, 111/12, 116/2, 4 etc.; **ȝour** *poss.* 83/23, 84/4; **your, yowre** 66/1, 67/16, 18, 78/1.

ȝede *pa.t. subj. sg.* should go 456/1.

ȝeelde *v.* give, pay back, render 36/9; **ȝeldesse** *pr. 3 sg.* 237/12; **yelde** *subj.* 9/2, 11/10; **ȝeldeys** *imp. pl.* 67/12; **ȝelde** *pa.t. 1 sg.* 395/5; **ȝeldede** *3 sg.* acknowledged 24/11; **ȝyeldede** produced 235/14; **ȝeldyne** *pp.* rendered 588/3; **ȝeelde** (*refl.*) submitted 171/14; **ȝolde** returned 408/20.

ȝeeldynge *vbl. n.* retribution 161/10.
ȝeuth *n.* early life *601/14; ȝowth 303/4.
ȝeve *v.* give 4/16; ȝiffene pr. pl. 480/21;
  yife *subj. sg.* 13/10; ȝave *pa.t. 3 sg.*
  15/16; yave 1/21, 4/17, 5/4, 7/1 etc.;
  yevene *pp.* 9/7; yooue 13/11.
ȝif *conj.* if 4/5, 50/9; yiff 11/15; ȝif(f) *alle*
  although 348/21, 370/17, 430/21.
ȝoylle *n.* Christmas 96/8, 100/21.
ȝoughthede *n.* youth 262/13-14; ȝowuthede
  86/3.

haate *adj.* ardent 89/10; warm 242/9.
haate *pp.* heated 89/8.
habbils see able *v.*
habyltye *n.* fitness 313/9.
habitacle *n.* dwelling place 569/7.
habyte *n.*; ∼ abbytte *of religioun* monastic
  profession 130/19, 566/15.
hadde *v.* add 134/15, 595/6.
haffe *v.* have 138/7; have 15/9; *(refl.)*
  behave, comport oneself 40/19, 53/11,
  169/20; betake oneself 120/1; hays *pr. 3*
  sg. has 331/17, 484/13; havesse 24/9;
  haffande *pr. p.* 461/2; hadde *pa.t. sg.* ([it]
  missing) 412/13; *subj.* should have
  510/21. Phr. ∼ *in excercyse* perform,
  practice 237/6-7, 250/4-5 etc.
hayle *adj.* steadfast 127/8; hayl(l)e healthy
  sound 297/10, 387/10; hoyle complete
  311/9.
hayle *adv.* completely, perfectly 230/1,
  280/19; hale 333/16; hole *30/11,
  102/3.
haylesome *adj.* wholesome 283/7; halsome
  83/4.
haylley *adv.* wholly 237/10; holye 188/21.
halfendele *n.* half 290/18.
halse *pr. 1 sg.* embrace 387/9, 10.
ham see be.
hame *n.* home 32/21.
hange see hynge.
hardynesse *n.* audacity, daring 76/14,
  458/18.
hasty *adj.* untimely 561/1.
hattreddene *n.* hatred 171/21.
hedderewarde *adv.* until now 115/8.
hee *pron.* he 41/13, 114/19, 461/3; hes
  poss. his 74/23, 539/19; his, hys its
  89/6, *239/6, 266/3, 282/17, 330/4;
  hym *dat.* it 173/12, 216/3, 547/10; *refl.*
  himself 10/8, 53/1, 56/20, 90/1, 8 etc.;
  itself 445/21.

heele *adj.* sound, healthy 480/12, 481/7.
heere *n.* hair 237/8, 286/21; herys *pl.*
  threads 226/13.
hegghede *pp.* surrounded 121/13, 122/13.
Heyle *n.* Elias 610/2.
heyle *n.* salvation, well-being 95/16, 98/22
  etc.
heylynge *vbl. n.* roofing 81/6; helienge
  clothing, covering 326/21; helynge
  112/15.
heyres see eyre.
heldeys *pr. 3 sg.* sheds 164/7; heeldeth
  pours 69/2, 92/1, 139/21; helde *pa.t.*
  sg. 138/1.
hele *v.* hide, keep secret 360/5; heylde *pa.t. 3*
  sg. covered over 173/13; helede 226/8.
hellys *pr. 3 sg.* pours 283/1.
herborede *pp.* lodged 150/12.
herdede *pp.* hardened 330/15.
here *pron. poss. pl.* their 3/2, 21, 22, 5/23,
  6/3, 7, 9 etc.; hem *acc. & dat.* 2/12,
  4/17, 5/9, 13, 12/16, 14/12 etc.
here *v.* hear, listen to 119/18, 242/21; hyere
  31/12, 43/3, 451/12, 15; hyre 115/18.
herynge *vbl. n.* glorification 77/2.
herne *n.* corner, hiding-place 348/17.
hertely, hertly *adj.* affectionate 227/3,
  388/15; hertlye *adv.* earnestly 134/12,
  433/2.
herteth *pr. 3 sg.* encourages, inspirits
  591/14.
hertye *adj.* steadfast 516/21.
hete *n.* inflammation 73/16.
hete *pron.* as *indef. subject* it 252/3.
hye *adj.* loud 253/21; rich in flavour
  217/17; exalted, sublime 3/9, 76/18,
  98/9, 13; *an* hie in heaven 367/2.
hyelye *adv.* solemnly 97/10, 241/23,
  325/15.
hynge *v.* hang 356/20; hange *pa.t. 3 sg.*
  264/5, 356/18; hynge 184/5.
holde *v.* hold, keep, maintain 4/9, 110/3;
  halde *refl.* adhere, cling 160/7; holdeys
  vp pr. 3 sg. supports 256/12; haldynge
  pr. p. esteeming 134/10; helde *pa.t. sg.*
  considered, regarded (as) 62/12, 67/3,
  74/3; haldene *pp.* 70/13; holdene
  obliged 478/7; restrained 356/9.
hole, hoyle see hayle.
homelye *adj.* kindly 223/22; hamelye familiar 486/11; homelye *adv.* intimately
  266/16, 602/6; hamelyere *comp.* 390/6.
homelyehede *n.* familiarity 318/17, 18.

homelynes(se), homlynesse *n.* intimacy 109/15, 243/15, 281/11.
honeste *adj.* neat 523/11; seemly 561/9.
hoope *n.* confidence 349/12.
hooste *n.* sacrifice 137/11, 12; consecrated wafer 254/12; **ooste** 254/14, 271/12.
hopede *pa.t. sg.*; ~*to* looked for 137/10.
hopenynge *vbl. n.* showing 508/6.
howe *adv.* however 72/19.
humours *n. pl.* fluids 325/20.

ignoraunce *n.* offence or sin caused by ignorance 277/3.
ylke *adj.* each, every 24/4, 435/20, 520/6.
impassibilite *n.* exemption from suffering 90/22.
implyede *pa.t. pl.* involved 580/5.
ympne *n.* hymn 97/8, 12, 427/14.
importunite *adj.* persistent 538/7.
in *prep.* among 78/13; for 65/5.
inclyne *pr. pl.* submit 267/13; **inclynede** *pa.t. sg.* disposed 205/10; bowed 23/17; **enclynede** 94/1.
inclynynges *vbl. n. pl.* bowings in worship 270/7-8; **enclynynge** 98/4.
informacion *n.* instruction 61/11, 583/11.
inhabytyde *pp.* domiciled 576/17.
inpungne *pr. subj. pl.* assail 346/8.
insomykelle, insomykylle *adv.* insomuch 336/13, 349/21, 413/3.
inspyre *v.* impart 472/16; **inspyrede** *pp.* divinely influenced or animated 60/13, 131/16.
into *prep.* as, for 192/17, 208/14, 16, 242/15 etc.; until 593/1.
inwardnes, inwardenes *n.* innermost part, interior nature 83/15, 184/19.
irene *n.* iron 176/1; *in* **yrene** by sword 231/16
yreouse *adj.* wrathful 161/13.
ysee *n.* ice 130/8.

Iame the Lasse *n.* James the Less 221/16-17.
Ieremye *n.* Jeremias 208/9.
ioe *n.* joy 596/5.
ioynedde *pp.* charged, enjoined 469/18.
Ionatha *n.* Jonathan 225/3.
iug(g)e *n.* judge 193/3, 401/16; **iewge** 168/16.
iugemente *n.*; *place of* ~ consistory 35/18, 390/9-10, 20.
iustifiede *pp.* absolved 391/23.

kele *pr. subj. sg.* cool 482/21.
kepere *n.* guardian 80/8, 204/20.
kynde *n.* natural state 130/9; *in* ~naturally 95/12; *in his* ~ by its nature 89/6; **kendys** *pl.* forms, species 373/7.
kynreden(e) *n.* kindred 108/20.
kyrke *n.* church 70/12, 219/3.
kysse *v.* kiss 94/18; **kesse** *imp. sg.* 176/12; **kusse** 176/6.
kyste *n.* coffin 177/15.
kyttynges *vbl. n. pl.* cuttings, pieces 604/13.
knawelechynge *vbl. n.* praise 109/13.
knawynge *vbl. n.* knowledge 61/15; acquaintance 84/10; **knawynges** *pl.* intimations 170/6; instructions 191/6.
knettynge *vbl. n.* pledge 547/8, 11.
knottes *n. pl.* rings 123/17.
knowelech *n.* acquaintance *566/2.
knoweleche *pr. 3 sg.* confess 295/12; **knawlechede** *pp.* acknowledged 149/6.
kombe *v.* comb 19/3; **keme** *imp. sg.* 262/4; **kembde** *pp.* (for *inf.*) 259/18.
kunnynge see **connynge**.

laarge *adj.* generous, munificent 171/21, 279/3, 402/5, 406/19; over-generous, prodigal 307/6, 7.
layth *adj.* repulsive 470/15.
lange *adv.* for a long time 143/18; **langere, langgere** *comp.* longer 70/22, 133/15.
langoorde *pa.t. pl.* languished 583/2.
langores *adj.* languishing 95/7.
largyce *n.* liberality 361/12, 17, 458/7.
lastynge *pr.p.* extending 143/4.
latanye *n.* litany 557/16; **letanye** 58/3, 506/13, 15, 557/12.
latune *n.* mixed metal of yellow colour 468/11.
lauour *n.* spiritual washing 178/15.
lawe *pr. subj. sg.* humble, lower 244/21; **lawede** *pa.t. 3 sg.* 462/2; **lowede** 241/5.
lawenes *n.* condescension 34/2; **lawnes** 379/13; baseness 112/9; **lownes** humility 67/3.
lawly(e), lawelye *adj.* humble 39/4, 76/16, 93/23, 169/12; **lowlye** 417/7, 586/17.
lecherye *n.* lewdness, lust 23/10; **lechorye** 61/8; **lycherye** 305/14, 19.
leefefulle *adj.* permitted 600/22; **leffulle** 521/9; **lefulle** 433/10.
legacye *n.* message 400/2.
lenynge-instrumente *n.* support 364/5.
lentyne *n.* Lent 604/8.

lerenynge *vbl. n.* instruction 298/5; **lernynge** 68/5, 526/1.

lesynge *n.* falsehood; *mayde* ... ~ told a lie 601/19.

lestene *v.* diminish 465/2.

lette *v.* hinder, prevent 269/6; **lette** *pp.* distracted 32/3, 46/8.

lettynge *vbl. n.* hindrance, obstacle 25/1, 246/10 etc.

letuarye *n.* electuary 228/3.

leuacion *n.* elevation of the Host 55/20, 540/2, 10.

leuere *adv. comp.*; *hadde* ~ would rather 428/15, 535/13-14.

leuynge *vbl. n.* stopping 533/6; see **lyuynge**.

levynge *vbl. n.* manner of life 41/16, 63/20; **lyevynge** 1/5, 42/1, 64/5.

ly(e) *v.* lie, rest 17/1; (*inf.* for *pr. p.*) 560/12; **ligge** 604/18.

lyche, lieche, lyeke *to quasi-prep.* like 3/11, 20/9, 50/6, 68/17 etc.

lyefe *n.* life 235/1; **leve** 55/12; *o, of, on(e)* **lyffe, lyue** alive 58/7, 206/5, 381/23, 479/2.

lyes *n. pl.* sediment 152/10.

lyevers *n. pl.* living persons 47/12; **lyuers** 186/3.

lyfe *v.* live 283/8; **lyue** 283/9; **lyevysse** *pr. 3 sg.* 220/14; **leuede** *pa.t. sg.* 212/12; **levydde** 41/13, 110/19; **lyevydde** 59/22.

lyght *adj.* bright 370/11.

lyȝt *n.*; *sette* ~ *be* account of small value 485/18.

lyghttenynge *vbl. n.* enlightenment 268/17.

lykes *pr. 3 sg.* pleases (with *dat.*) 298/16.

lykynge *adj.* agreeable 324/15; plump 363/22, 364/1.

lykyng(e)lye *adv.* pleasantly 492/20, 602/6; with pleasure 390/2.

lymys, lymmes *n. pl.* members (of the Church) 149/17, 189/18.

lynne *adj.* linen 238/8.

liquifiede *pp. adj.* "melted" with spiritual ardour 79/19.

lytelle *adv.* slightly 51/16; ~ *ande* ~ a little at a time 145/5.

lyuelye *adj.* living 132/11.

lyuynge *adj.* living 294/7; **lyffynge** 452/3; **leuynge** flowing 229/16.

loythes *pr. 3 sg.* is unwilling 210/12; **loyth** *subj. no man* ~ *hitt* let no one be displeased with it 611/9; **loythede** *pp.* detested 378/19.

loovynge *vbl. n.* praise 352/19, 392/4, 415/2 etc.

loue *pr. 1 sg.* praise 445/4.

lowlye *adv.* abjectly 586/14; condescendingly 381/13; **lawlye** reverently 169/18.

luffelye *adj.* loving 313/19, 413/18; **lufflye** 332/20.

luffesome *adj.* loving 576/18.

mayke *v.* make, cause, do 124/6, 298/3; **mayde** *pa.t. sg. & pl.* 167/9, 299/4. Phr. ~ *confessyone* confess 39/12-13; ~ *cleere* enlighten 256/7; ~ *alle oone* unite 79/21-22, 214/7 etc.

maystrye *n.* dominion *608/20, 608/21.

maner(e) *n.* custom, practice 111/22, 166/19; sg. form after numbers 15/5, 7, 26/3, 152/4; without following *of* kind of 42/6, 95/3, 164/14 etc.; ~ *kyndes* kinds 57/7.

mare see **more**.

marowh *n.* essence, inmost part 95/6, 567/23.

maste see **moste** *adj.*

mateere *n.* cause, reason 160/10, 548/7; **matier** fuel (fig.) 303/3.

meddelede, meddelyd, medlede (*amonge, emonge*) *pp.* mixed with 148/14-15, 258/13, 19.

mees *n.* prepared dish, serving of food 151/7, 22; **meyse(s)** *pl.* 188/12, 189/12, 13; **messe** 12/17; **messys** 361/15, 19.

meyne *n.* family 303/15.

mekelle *adj.* great 346/6.

melte *v.* languish 235/5; become soft, dissolve 431/15; **molte(ne)** *pp.* 216/1, 5, 226/15, 229/23.

mene *n.* mediator 608/2; *withoute* ~ directly 609/18-19.

menetyme, meynetyme *n.*; *in þat* (*this*) ~ at the same time 226/6, 381/10-11, 408/17, 588/1.

merke *imp. sg.* bless (yourself) 446/1.

mervelydde, merveyllede *pa.t. sg.* wondered 288/5, 371/22; **meruellede** *of* marvelled at 102/20.

meruelys *adj.* marvellous 166/9; **meruelous** 75/21.

message *n.* mission 51/12; conversation 381/4; *dydde his* ~ delivered his tidings 312/18.

messe see **mees**.

mete *n.* food 223/15, 228/3, 232/10, 11;

metis, metys *pl.* dishes 8/17, 44/4, 150/4.

meuewe, mevedde see **move.**

mevynge *vbl. n.* movement, pulse 3/12; **mouynge** 101/5.

myght *n.*; *fulle ~* omnipotence 128/3, 131/18, 154/2.

myrtiene *n.* myrtle 177/4.

myschefe *n.* distress, trouble 462/8, 606/20.

myscheuouse *adj.* miserable 391/10.

mysseesydde *adj.* distressed 582/13.

mysspekynge *vbl. n.* calumny 113/9.

mystryste *pr. subj. 2 sg.* be doubtful 545/9; *3* despair 517/10.

mo(o) *adj. comp.* more (in number) 37/21, 67/2, 130/12, 406/9.

moche *adv.*; *als (as) ~as in (one) (is, was)* as much as (one) (is, was) able 66/21, 264/18-19, 313/7-8, 539/12.

modelacion *n.* intonation 141/9.

moderlye *adj.* befitting a mother 241/21.

Moyses *n.* Moses 612/3, 4.

moyste see **more** *adv.*

moneth *n.* month 58/21; *alle a ~* a whole month 33/19, 379/7.

more *adv. comp.* more (pleonastically) 75/10, 387/13; **mare** 351/16, 400/17; **moyste** *sup.* mostly 550/19, 19.

moste *adj.*[1] *sup.* greatest 6/10, 8/9; **maste** 492/1; *~thynge* chief thing 524/2.

moste *adj.*[2] saturated 217/12.

moste *pr. 1 sg.* must 307/6; *2* 373/13; *3* 100/14, 485/11, 499/13; *pl.* 398/12.

mote, motte *subj. sg. & pl.* may 194/1, 227/13.

move *v. refl.* stir 99/5, 12-13; **meuewe** *pr. subj. sg.* remind 309/3; **mouynge** *pr. p.* beating 102/18; **movyde** *of pa.t. sg.* proceeded from 103/4; **mevedde** *pp.* roused, stirred up 396/17; **mouede** provoked to anger 536/3.

mow(e) *v.* be able to 280/15, 286/17; **maiste** *pr. 2 sg.* 222/19; **mayste** 409/19, 20; **may** *3 sg.* 11/12, 175/21; **mowe** *pl.* 175/11, 12; *subj.* 43/2, 82/22, 97/11; **might, myght** *pa.t. sg.* 27/1, 47/7, 50/8, 12; *subj.* 7/9, 10/5.

mowht *n.* mouth 107/8.

multiplyenge *vbl. n.* unnecessary increase 600/9.

na *adj.* no 504/4; *adv.* 46/5.

namelye *adv.* especially 362/10, 594/8, 607/17.

necessyte *n.*; *for a grete ~* because of serious circumstances 509/15.

nedelynges *adv.* necessarily 245/1.

neygh *v.* approach, draw near 234/2; **neyght** 278/7; **neyghe** (without *prep.*) 440/2; **neyghtynge** *pr. p.* (for *inf.*) 269/15; **neyhthede** *pp.* 317/8.

neythere *adj.* lower 22/3; **nedere** 288/17; **nethereste** *sup.* 434/13.

nemenynge *vbl. n.* naming 577/11.

nempne *v.* express 270/18; **nemenede** *pp.* named 58/3, 556/5 etc.

nesche *adj.* soft 328/19, 330/16, 17.

neuere *adv.* not at all 339/16.

nyht *adv.* near 43/2; **neghe** (with *dat.*) 246/11; **neght** 239/10,' 17; **nyght** 315/6.

no *conj.* nor 33/19, 36/12, 550/17.

nobyleye *n.* nobility, rank 288/21; **nobleye** noble birth 524/16.

noght *n.* nothing 334/3; **nowȝt** 126/22; *brouȝt to* **nought** destroyed 236/6; *of* **noȝt** of no value 586/6. See **sett.**

noye *v.* harass 345/7; harm 346/3.

noyes *n. pl.* annoyances, troubles 298/4.

none *n.* none (canonical hour of the daily office) 10/19, 167/15, 380/15.

nootede *pp.* obliterated; *~ in hereselfe* insensible 357/10-11.

norysche *v.* feed 153/6; **noryschede** *pa.t. sg.* cherished 137/22; **nuryschede** nurtured 425/12.

nosestrellys *n. pl.* nostrils 422/6.

nothynge *adv.* in no way 370/16.

nower whare *adv.* nowhere 343/10.

nowht *adv.* not 485/2, 587/1, 592/5.

nowthere *adv.*; *~ ... ne, nor* neither ... nor 71/22-23, 144/14-15, 524/15-16.

o, oo *adj.* one 4/12, *101/5, 102/19; **on** 353/5, 467/11; **aane** 379/3.

obrede see **abrode** .

of, off *prep.* for 54/22, 348/8, 442/19, 575/11; from, out of 9/16, 12/17, 21/21, 27/23, 29/23; in, as regards 54/12, 63/10, 69/22, 113/9; with 192/7, 9, 413/16; among 510/3; over 297/15; *~ (one) selfe* by (one's) own power 197/4, 357/11.

of alle see **thowe.**

office, offyce *n.* introit of the Mass 6/8, 18/14 etc.

ofte sithes (sythes, sythis) *adv.* oftentimes 45/6, 48/20, 54/16.

on *prep.* against 10/13; in 5/3; **one** 67/12; on 9/14, 17/10 etc.; **oo** (apocopate form) during 101/9.

onys *adv.* once 285/9; *atte* ~simultaneously 158/11.

oone *v.* unite 531/8; **oynnede** *pp.* 466/20.

ooste see **hooste**.

opene *adj.* exposed, uncovered 55/16; evident 350/15.

openeth *pr. 3 sg.* penetrates 372/10; **opyne** *subj.* expose 493/21; **oponyd** *pa.t. pl.* pierced 165/18.

openlye *adv.* publicly 119/16; clearly 356/11.

or *conj.* before 24/8, 29/8, 42/11 etc.; **ore** or 39/21; **ar** 579/6.

ordeyns *pr. 3 sg.* arranges 462/14; **ordeyne** *here subj.* set herself 383/18; **ordeyned(e)** *pa.t. sg.* ordered 103/10; determined 59/4; *pl.* prepared 150/11; *pp.* destined 7/4, 5; assigned 156/8, 170/6.

ordere *n.* divine service 47/8, 482/10, 19; monastic rule 18/16, 148/19.

ornamente *n.* trappings 252/18; brooch 253/11, 17.

otterlye *adv.* entirely 261/18, 338/10; truly, sincerely 238/11.

ottewarde *adj.* external 603/2.

ouere *adj.* upper 22/3, 30/20; **ouereste** *sup.* outermost 326/22.

ouere *prep.* in addition to 238/16; beyond 257/21; ~*euen* on the preceding evening 314/11.

ouereallewhare *adv.* everywhere 603/11.

ouerepasse *pr. subj. pl.* leave unnoticed 422/3.

ouerepassynge *adj.* surpassing 184/21.

our(e), owre *n.* hour 10/17, 18, 168/16, 181/7, 187/17; **owrys** *pl.* 45/13, 20.

owꝫt *adv.* out 338/1, 12.

owght *n.* anything whatever 451/22.

owhere *adv.* anywhere *487/13.

owthere *adv.*; ~... *or* either ... or 73/14-15, 185/6.

owthere *pron.* any one else 71/23; **othere** *pl.* 14/6, 21/2, 63/2; **odere** 527/6.

owtlaurye *n.* exile 110/1.

paleys *n.* palace 84/18.

pallyoun *n.* cloak 203/6.

pamente *n.* floor 377/15.

parte *pr. 1 sg.* impart 231/3; *pl.* share 231/18.

Paske *n.* Easter 13/13, 31/7; **Passe** 13/6.

passibilite *n.* passibility, capability of suffering *90/20.

passynge *adj.* surpassing 2/15, 85/11; temporal 95/19; *adv.* exceedingly 182/18.

peese *n.* pea 371/15.

peese *v.* appease 496/14.

pelews *n. pl.* pillows 383/1.

penalite, penalyte *n.* suffering 388/13, 469/7; **penalte** 45/15.

peresch *v.* pass away, perish 516/22; **perrysche** *pr. subj. sg.* go astray, be lost 549/8; **peryche** *pl.* 120/7.

peresede *adj.* perforated 546/12.

performe, perfourme *v.* accomplish 353/8; carry out, complete 65/11, 91/3; satisfy 352/8; make good 351/5; *pr. subj. sg.* perfect 104/4, 157/10; **performede** *pp.* supplied 511/7.

perseth *pr. 3 sg.* pierces 452/13, 583/21; **peryscheth** 438/20; **peresede** *pa.t. sg.* 377/19; **persede** moved deeply 103/12.

pystylle *n.* epistle 252/19; **pystelle** 329/14.

playne *adj.* even 573/20.

platys *n. pl.* sheets (of metal) 183/19.

pleyere *n.* performer 199/13.

pleynede *pa.t. sg.* made complaint 429/8; *refl.* lamented 34/23.

plesaunde *adj.* pleasing 294/13.

plese *v.* delight, gratify 11/12; **pleyses** *pr. 3 sg.* 149/7; **pleyseys** 551/21; **plesis** *hitt* it is pleasing 66/9; **pleyseth** does it please 149/6; *me* ~it pleases me 528/2.

plyete *n.* condition 439/13.

poort *n.* external deportment 606/1.

potestates *n. pl.* order of angels (powers) 138/21, 239/15.

poure *absol.* poor people 306/21.

pouse, pows(e) *n.* pulse 3/11, 101/4, 102/16, 19.

powere *n.*; *haffe* ~ be able 551/10; *in* ~ under control 245/16; *of none* ~ *of thyselfe* unable by yourself 197/4; *to his* ~ as far as he is able 47/22-23, 486/5, 521/18.

preciouslye *adv.* exceedingly 243/19. See Note.

preciouste *n.* costliness 162/15.

preferre *v.* prefer 502/3; *pr. 1 sg.* advance, promote 528/2; *subj. sg.* hold in esteem 75/9.

presente *n.*; *in* ~in the presence 213/23.

presume *(of) pr. 3 pl.* rely upon *418/17.

pryce, prys(e) *n.* excellence 515/9; value

193/1, 271/15; cost, price 192/17, 212/20; **priece** 190/4; *be sette on a ~* estimated 547/9.

principatys *n. pl.* order of angels (principalities) 138/21.

pryntede *pa.t. sg.* pressed 79/5.

priuetees *n. pl.* secrets 67/2; **priuetes** divine mysteries 107/15.

procure *v.* labour 353/18.

profettys *n. pl.* prophets 472/13.

profitable, profytable *quasi-adv.* advantageously 515/4-5, 564/16; **profetable** 473/21.

profyte, profytte *n.* advantage, benefit 37/18, 39/2; **profette** 47/2; **prophite** 218/9; *to ~*for use 489/15.

profyte *v.* improve, make progress 237/17; **profytes** *pr. 3 sg.* does good to 308/1; avails 43/3; **prophites** *pl.* 573/3.

propyrlye *adv.* particularly, specially 196/20, 201/21; **propurlye** strictly speaking 606/16.

psawterye *n.* stringed instrument 35/20; **psawtrye** 392/17; **psawtere** 392/13.

pure *adj.* unmixed, unalloyed 30/16; **puere** 146/19, 166/7.

puredde *adj.* refined 358/4.

purpoyse *v. (refl.)* resolve 297/21; **purposes** *pl.* (ellip.) are bound to come 288/13.

purpore *n.* purple color 112/7; **purpure** purple stone 37/12, 404/2, 18.

purueye *pr. 3 sg.* arranges beforehand 146/2; **purueyde** *pa.t. sg.* foresaw *261/2.

putt(e) *v.* place 88/3; *(refl.)* subject (oneself) 385/21; **puttede** *pa.t. pl.* added 296/22. Phr. *~agaynes* charge 171/4; *~awaye* get rid of 240/8-9; cast out, drive away 267/4; *~ behynde* disregard 343/5; *~ fro(me)* divert, turn away from 323/15; *~ offe* prevent 523/6.

qwele *n.* small tube 255/2.

qwere *n.* choir 7/17, 12/14, 148/4.

qwycke *v.* stir up, inspire 501/9.

qwyk(e) *adj.* flowing, running 222/4, 229/16, 282/11.

qwyte *adj.* clear, free 61/13, 583/13.

raysynge *pr. p.* scratching 582/12.

raythere, rayþer *adv.* rather 425/16; *the* **rathere** more readily 548/12.

rauenour *n.* robber 287/1.

rawe *n.; on ~*in a line *93/1.

reboundynge *vbl. n.* superfluity 248/2.

receyte *n.* admittance 434/20.

receyue, receyve *v.* accept, take 69/6; **resayve** 1/20; **ressaffe** *pr. subj. pl.* 328/3; **resseve** 69/1; **reseyvede** *pp.* swallowed up (fig.) 336/12; **receyuede** *(auxil.* missing) 602/23.

receyuynge *vbl. n.* ; *~place* dwelling 14/23-15/1, 215/3-4, 10.

recyte *v.* receive *135/5.

recreacion *n.* comfort 257/4, 607/9.

redynge *vbl. n.* ; *in ~* being read 110/9, 273/15.

redressynge *pr. p.* directing 303/8.

reede *v.* read 27/6, 337/13; **radde** *pp.* 361/2.

refuete *n.* refuge 458/17; **refute** 210/15, 306/21.

regalye *n.* royalty 125/3.

reysede *pa.t. sg.* restored 109/16.

relees *pr. 1 sg.* remit 443/20; **relese** mitigate 443/21.

relygione, relygioun *n.* monastic life 1/4, 70/5; religious rule 73/9.

religious, relygious(e) *adj.* bound by monastic vows 18/5, 50/17, 57/17.

relygiouste *n.* monastic life 244/13.

remove *v.* move, persuade 72/1; **remevede** *pp.* 350/1.

renne *v.* run 90/7, 91/1; **rynne** *pr. subj. pl.* let us run 125/4; **renne** *pp.* flowed 430/1.

rennynge *vbl. n.* flowing 595/20; **rynnynge** 230/1.

renuynge *vbl. n.* newness 439/15.

replenschynge *vbl. n.* fullness 292/3, 370/15.

represente *v.* present, show 509/21.

reprofe *n.; hadde ... in ~*scorned 470/6-7; **reprofeys** *pl.* insults 207/3; **reprovys** 112/14.

reredde *pp.* lifted 371/14.

resonable *adv.* with good reason 587/13.

respon(e) *n.* responsory 14/10, 148/3.

restore *v.* make amends for 161/7.

reue *v.* deprive 245/1.

reuerence *n.; atte (the) ~of* out of respect for 106/10, 469/14; *do(o) ~to* honor, show respect for 9/11.

reuokede *pp.* drawn away 349/22.

rewarde *n.* recompense 27/23; *haffynge ~to* in comparison with 145/9, 485/19.

rewle *n.* monastic rule 185/17.

rialle, ryalle *adj.* royal 146/20, 388/5.

ryalle *adv.* royally, splendidly 112/4; **ryallye** 125/2.

ryde *adj.* right 243/5.

ryechelye *adv.* splendidly, sumptuously 121/11.

ryght *adv.* very 75/14; exactly, just 79/20; *rygh,* ~ *nought* nothing at all 145/9, 177/10, 227/3-4.

ryghtwysnes *n.* justice 1/7, 65/2.

ryse *v.* recover from a spiritual fall 155/13; **rayse** *pa.t. sg.* stood up 32/7, 46/21, 93/22; **royse** 273/12; **rase** *pl.* 105/3, 4.

rodye *adj.* ruddy *340/14, 457/4.

rodynesse *n.* ruddy complexion 456/20.

roystede *adj.* roasted 151/20; **rostede** 583/6.

roote *n.* foot (of a hill) 34/11, 383/10, 19.

roote *v.* decay, die 184/3.

rowȝh *adj.* bristly 573/21; **rowhȝ** 574/3.

rownnynges *n. pl.* private conversations 230/6.

sacrarye *n.* temple 261/20.

sacrynge *vbl. n.* consecration (of the Mass) 32/7, 369/9.

sadde *adj.* firm, steadfast 349/12, 368/11, 500/3; *adv.* thoroughly 347/11.

safe *adj.* spiritually "whole" 234/12.

saffynge *prep.* without prejudice to 585/11.

saght, saugh(t) see **see.**

saghthelde, saghthylde *pa.t. sg.* assuaged 121/7, 356/2; **sawhtelde** 121/2.

sal, salle *pr. 1, 3 sg. & pl.* shall 124/6, 134/9, 228/3; **schalle** 11/8, 10 etc.; **schulde** *pa.t. sg.* was about to 1/19, 12/2, 7, 15/21 etc.

sare see **sore.**

Sawle-Messe *n.;* ~ *daye* All Souls' Day 59/20.

sawtez *n. pl.* assaults 159/8, 9.

schape *pr. 1 sg.* plan 175/1; **schappyne** *pp.* formed 402/10.

scharpe *adj.* bristly 573/20.

scharpelye *adv.* swiftly 145/4.

schedes *pr. 3 sg.* sheds 531/6; **schydes** 531/6; **schadde** *pa.t. pl.* 272/7.

schellys *n. pl.* fragments 604/13.

Scher(e) Thursday(e) *n.* Thursday in Holy Week 9/14, 157/18.

schettynge *vbl. n.* support 364/7.

schydes see **schedes** .

schrynes *n. pl.* caskets, reliquaries 319/4.

see *n.* seat of authority 2/14.

see *v.* see 65/5; **seys** *pr. 3 sg.* 213/15; **saght** *pa.t. sg.* 325/16, 326/5; **saugh(t)** 13/20, 15/11, 14, 16/2 etc.; **seie** *pp.* 584/3; **syene** 183/22; **syne** foreseen 207/7.

seke *v.* seek, search for 48/1; **syekys** *pr. pl.* 269/13; **sought** *pa. t. 1 & 3 sg.* 198/8, 378/4; **sowȝth** *pl.* 164/15; **soght, sowȝt** (*oute*) *pp.* examined, fathomed 204/16, 241/22.

selfe *adj.* same 283/10, 377/15.

sellere *n.* spice chest (fig.) 464/8.

semblaunte *n.* countenance 128/4, 456/15; appearance, look 284/19, 20, 22.

semelyehede *n.* seemliness 524/18; pleasing appearance 134/20; **semelyede** 503/13.

semeth *pr. 3 sg.* is seen 89/5; **semynge** *pr. p.* it seeming 611/6; **semede** *pa.t. sg.* was suitable 147/4; *hitt* **semydde** *here* she seemed 73/11; *here* ~ it seemed to her 94/17, 235/2, 253/23-24 etc.

semynge *vbl. n.* ; *to here* ~as it seemed to her 12/3, 18/9, 28/4, 78/7 etc.; *to* ~to all appearance 217/17, 290/18.

sengynge *adj.* ? bubbling, burning 339/15. See Note.

sentence *n.* opinion, way of thinking 69/10; gist, meaning 181/14, 562/20.

sett(e) *v.* place 9/8; (*inf.* for *pr. p.*) caring 425/6; *pa.t. sg.* estimated 599/2; **settede** (*refl.*) sat 557/10; **settyne** *pp.* sat down 249/14. Phr. ~ *al(l) abowte* surround 53/23, 172/11; ~ *att(e) nought* despise 84/1, 218/16; ~ (*one's*) *affecioun, desyres, herte, mynde* center (one's) feelings, thoughts 33/18, 163/7, 233/11, 267/18.

sewere *n.* attendant at a meal 459/7.

syeke *v.* grow sick 556/6.

syekenes *n.* illness, physical suffering 33/20, 34/6; *in his* **syeknesse** at the point of death 58/13.

syekere, sykere *adj.* certain, assured 176/16, 197/2; safe 458/17.

syen, sien *conj.* since 119/18, 153/9, 185/3; **seyne** 210/13, 396/8.

syghchynge *vbl. n.* sighing 413/4; **syhthynges** *pl.* 359/8.

syghȝe *pr. subj. sg.* sigh 521/17; **syghynge** (*pr. p.* for *inf.*) 83/11.

sight, syght *n.* opinion 73/1; *to* ~to the eye 243/7, 392/13; *to here* ~it seemed to her 89/2-3, 90/5, 92/15, 105/17-18 etc.

syke *adj.* ailing 557/10; **syeke** 34/23; **seke** 387/9; **seeke** 386/17 etc.; morally corrupt 297/10.

synfulle *n. pl.* sinful persons 539/9.

syonys *n. pl.* branches 330/2, 6.

sithes, sythis *n. pl.* times 11/9, 15/18, 46/10 etc.

syttynge *pr. p.* dwelling 609/6; (for *inf.*) sit 292/10.

skylfulle *adj.* reasonable, right 600/15.

skochynys *n. pl.* escutcheons, shields 221/2.

slawe see **slowe** *adj.*

slewth(e) *n.* sloth, sluggishness 23/11, 41/11, 54/17, 69/22; **slewht** 578/2.

slyke *adj.* such 66/17, 70/1, 372/16, 384/11, 426/10 etc.

slo *n.* slough 582/18, 18.

slokende, slokenede *pp.* quenched 228/15, 356/18.

slowe *adj.* slothful, sluggish 26/12, 335/13, 18; **slawe** 572/4.

slowe *pa.t. 3 sg.* put to death 372/15.

slugerye *n.* sluggishness 303/4.

sluggye *adj.* sluggish 454/10.

smalle *adj.* fine 262/3; ~ *and gentelle* graceful 90/3; **smayle** small 283/12.

smertynge *vbl. n.* sharp pain 604/17.

smyllynge *adj.* smelling 484/8.

sodyne *pp.* boiled 605/4; **sodeyn** *adj.* 605/3.

softelye *adj.* pleasant 263/12, 281/12.

soyth *n.* truth 232/7.

solle *n.* soul 598/17.

somewhate *n.* some portion 452/18.

soote *adj.* sweet *572/5.

soppys *n. pl.* pieces of bread dipped in water or wine 249/21.

sore *adv.* excessively 28/19, 34/22, 40/3; painfully 73/16, 162/3; eagerly, earnestly 31/21; closely, tightly 45/9, 79/5; **sare** 377/17.

sorowhede *pa.t. sg.* lamented 409/2.

soth *adj.* true 45/24, 61/21, 84/15; **soyth** 473/4.

sotylle *adj.* acute, subtle 107/7.

sowke *v.* suck 353/14.

sowne *v.* sound 31/22; ? appear 134/19, see Note.

sownynge *adj.* sonorous 73/8.

speciouste, specyouste *n.* beauty, fair appearance 81/1, 94/3.

sperede *pp.* in ~*owte* excluded 224/17.

spowsehede *n.* espousal 227/11.

sprynges, spryngges *n. pl.* shoots, sprigs 9/16, 157/20.

sprynges *pr. 3 sg.* flows 352/21.

spryngeth *pr. 3 sg.* sprinkles 484/6; **sprengede** *pa.t. sg.* 214/21, 220/19; **spreneyde** 263/14; **sprengide** *pp.* bespattered 147/17.

sterenesse *n.* severity 189/2.

sterne *n.* star 310/22, 311/2.

stye *n.* ladder 265/4, 266/5.

styede *pr. 3 sg.* ascended 205/19.

stillede, styllede *pa.t. pl.* hung down 139/19; distilled 322/1.

styllynge *vbl. n.* trickling 322/4.

styrre *v.* move, incite 77/15; **sterres** *pr. 3 sg.* 413/7.

stodye *pr. subj. sg.* endeavor 112/22; *pl.* (~ *we*) let us try 439/20; *imp. sg.* set yourself 305/6; **studyede** *pa.t. sg.* deliberated 276/12.

stokkys *n. pl.* tree stumps 372/3.

stole *n.* throne 27/15, 339/2; footstool 339/9.

stone *n.* gall-stone 73/15; gem 5/19; **stanes** *pl.* 447/21, 449/11.

stonynge *vbl. n.* amazement 93/21.

stowte *adj.* fierce 525/21.

straykede see **strekynge**.

straytelye, strayttelye *adv.* strictly 161/20, 298/6; tightly 356/9.

streyght *adv.*; *evene* ~ directly, immediately 573/15.

streyght *pa.t. sg.* extended, stretched 120/17, 273/22.

streyʒte *adv.* tightly 423/6; **straytere** *comp.* 91/5; more closely 390/2.

streyte *adj.*[1] erect 90/2.

streyte *adj.*[2] severe, strict 495/3.

strekynge *pr. p.* stretching 496/11; **straykede** *pa.t. sg.* 411/18.

studiosyte *n.* careful attention 300/11.

sudarye *n.* humeral veil 254/15; shroud 598/5.

sufferynge *adj.* long-suffering, submissive 305/18.

sugette *adj.* exposed 192/5; subordinate, submissive 151/10, 262/15 etc.

sugette *n.* subject 169/12.

suppoyse, suppose *v.* imagine 563/12; *als itt es to* ~as we believe 369/20-21.

suscepcion *n.* undertaking 312/16.

suspendede *pa.t. pl.* interdicted 251/20.

susteyne *v.* support 364/6; **susteneys** *pr. 3 sg.* *256/10.

swa *adv.* so 591/10.

swiche, swyche *adj.* such 107/9, 227/16, 313/15; **swhiche** 321/16; **swilke, swylke** 337/9, 399/14.

swolwyde *pp.* ? closely united 225/3. See Note.

talentys *n. pl.* (fig.) riches, treasure 267/10.

tarryede *pp.* harrassed, worried 428/19; **terryede** 571/10.

teyne *v.* (without *prep.*) attend, direct oneself (to) 297/21; **tendede** *pa.t. 3 sg.* 381/9; *pp.* 374/9.

tempre *v.* (*refl.*) restrain oneself 532/1; **temprede** *pp.* blended 304/21.

tente *v.* give heed 433/6.

termynede *pp.* declared 281/16.

thare, þare *adv.* where 33/7, 118/21, 213/15, 280/22 etc.

þareagayns *adv.* in opposition to that 305/15.

þareto *adv.* besides 595/6.

tharewith, þarewith *adv.* following upon that 26/15, 226/7; together with that 266/6, 468/8.

þase *adj. pl.* those 558/21; **thoos** 31/21.

thay, þay *pron. pl.* they 3/18, 19, 4/5, 6/1, 9, 12/17, 14/14 etc.; **thare(e), þare** *poss.* 30/5, 65/10, 88/14, 125/18, 20, 21, 22 etc.; **there** 2/9, 10, 17/12, 43/10; **þaame** *acc. & dat.* 373/10, 410/5; **thaym, þaim, þaym** 23/2, 107/20, 120/6; **thame, þame** 6/2, 19, 50/8, 58/6; *refl.* themselves 6/16, 32/20, 43/9 etc.

the *pron. pl.* those 93/4; **tho(o), þo** 6/15, 67/9, 69/6 etc.

þees *adj. sg.* this 166/8; **thes** 213/10; *pl.* these 5/3, 25/10; **this, thys** 31/19, 68/11, 77/20, 186/4.

thenke *v.* conceive, think 48/10, 74/23; **thynke** 54/2, 212/18; *to ~ þareof* (*inf.* for *pr. p.*) by thinking on it 517/5-6.

þere *adj. pl.* these 216/12, 407/8, 416/14.

thynke *pr. impers.* in *hym ~* it seems to him 535/13.

tho(o), þoo *adj. pl.* those 5/23, 12/18, 19, 14/18, 20, 16/21 etc.

thowe, þowe *conj.* though 68/4, 163/8; even if 137/15; *of alle* (apocopate form) even though 426/20.

thredde, þredde *adj.* third 410/16, 416/17.

threde, þrede *n.* fabric other than silk 90/10; thread 482/5.

threstede *pa.t. sg.*[1] longed for 356/16; **thrystede** 176/18.

threstede, þrestede *pa.t. sg.*[2] pressed 354/13; *pp.* pushed, thrust 162/4.

thretynge *vbl. n.* threatening 71/23.

thrystes *pr. 3 sg.* thrusts 545/3.

tylle *prep.* to 359/19, 419/7.

tyme *n.*; *fro ~ to ~* from day to day, continuously 72/4, 286/14; *laste ~* period immediately preceding the Last Judgment 612/1, 9.

tittere, tytter(e) *adv. comp.* sooner 375/14, 17, 436/2, 575/3, 607/20.

to *conj.* until 274/2, 294/16, 339/21; *prep.* before 3/16, 27/12; for 13/12, 20/12, 27/12 etc.; from 205/12; in 73/10, 89/19, 143/6 etc.; in the presence of 4/10, 110/4, 11, 152/9 etc.; with 608/18; with regard to 28/5, 341/9.

to-brostene *pp.* broken apart 604/16.

toffoore *adv.* previously 336/2; **tofore** 144/19.

tofore *prep.* before 3/14, 6/4, 8/15 etc.; **toforn** 10/12.

tofornesaide *adj.* previously mentioned 12/19.

togedders *adv.* each other 116/13; mutually 181/22, 283/19, 22; **togeders** consecutively 3/11.

togeder *adv.* uninterruptedly 336/19; **togedyre** 26/20; **togyddere** 336/7.

toone *adj.* one 354/12.

to-rente *pp.*; *alle ~* lacerated 343/21, 344/11; torn 602/14.

tother(e), toþer *adj.* other 110/14, 274/6, 401/20; (*absol.*) second 410/15.

travelle *v.* exert oneself 22/17; **trauaylles** *pr. 2 pl.* labour, work hard 116/1; **y-trauaylede** *pp.* harassed, troubled 28/19.

tretablye *adv.* with moderation 120/5.

trye *n.* dry land 328/18.

tryntalle *n.* set of thirty requiem Masses 561/19.

tryste *n.* confidence, faith 337/15.

Troiane *n.* Trajan *59/18.

trone *n.* throne 2/21, 20/5; **throni, throny** *pl.* third order of angels 239/8, 317/9.

trought *n.* plighted word 42/17; **trowth(e)** 447/19; belief 208/10.

trowe *v.* imagine, suppose 151/17; **troweth**

pr. 3 sg. believes, has confidence 69/3; **trowys** *3 pl.* 39/7.

trumpe, trumppe *n.* hollow tube 25/21, 325/10, 328/5, 7, 9.

tunacle *n.* tunicle, vestment resembling the dalmatic 187/22; **tunakelle** 28/8; **tunycle** 342/10, 15.

twelle see **dwelle**.

vnavysede *adv.* unexpectedly 168/3.

vnbynddynge *vbl. n.* absolution *394/4.

vnbynde *v.* absolve 509/5.

vndernyme *v.* rebuke 120/6.

vnderstondynge *adj.* intelligent 452/6.

vndertakere *n.* helper 171/10.

vndertoke *pa.t. 1 sg.* became surety (for), made me answerable (for) 355/14.

vndewlye *adv.* unrightfully 149/17.

vndisposede *adj.* unfitted 431/17.

vnede, vnydde *pp.* united 214/7, 467/12.

vneythes *adv.* scarcely 337/1; **vnnethis** 27/1; **vnneþs** 586/8; **vnnethes** with difficulty 606/5.

ungettene *adj.* unbegotten 393/11.

vngoodelye *adv.* roughly 425/8.

vnhele *pr. subj. sg.* disclose 523/14.

vnhurte *adj.* uncorrupted 191/20.

vnlustynes(se) *n.* disinclination, lukewarmness 441/1, 578/3.

vnmeuable *adj.* steadfast 316/21.

vnperfyte *adj.* incomplete 157/15.

vnsauoury *adj.* (fig.) lukewarm 431/17, 463/13.

vnto *prep.* until 523/10.

vntowchede *adj.* chaste 81/22.

vnwittynge, vnwyttynge *adj.* without the knowledge of 37/17, 65/15; *here* ~ unaware 603/4.

vse *n.* custom; *hadde the* ~*of* used 170/22; *haffe ... in* ~practice 474/11; *be takene into the* ~become habitual 473/14.

vse *v.* act 415/1; treat familiarly 470/21; *refl.* conduct (oneself) 473/21; *pr. subj. sg.* put into practice 41/8, 54/7; *pl.* 18/4; **vsede** *pa.t. sg.* dealt with 144/14; performed 608/22.

vttereste *n.* utmost 528/14.

veyne *adj.* empty, worthless 375/4, 424/15; *in* **vayn** casually, lightly 577/8.

veyne *n.* vein, water-course (fig.) 270/22, 23, 385/5, 12, 13; **vyne** 34/18.

venye *n.* the gesture of prostration as indication of penitence 492/22.

vermeloune *n.* scarlet color 139/17; **vermylune** 405/2.

verray(e) *adj.* real, true 72/17, 280/18; **verre** 23/4, 6, 134/8; **verrey** 22/17, 84/2.

verre, verrey *adv.* truly 296/16, 297/8, 18.

verteue *n.* power, might 372/2; **vertue** 77/14, 95/14, 101/18; moral excellence, virtue 59/15; (personification) 3/3; **vertewe** 22/15; **verteus** *pl.* 327/10; **vertues** extraordinary things 372/16.

vertues *adj.* commendable, praiseworthy 179/12, 220/2, 287/20; **vertuose** 73/2.

vyene *n.* vineyard 15/10; **vyne** 219/11.

vyole *n.* phial, small vessel 227/23.

visitacion *n.* comforting presence or influence 27/4; **vysitacions** *pl.* trials 73/17.

vysite *v.* go in order to worship 6/5; **vysitede, vysytede** *pp.* enriched 31/8, 73/12; comforted 26/21, 36/21.

voyce *n.* report 396/15.

voyde *adj.* empty-handed 250/18; empty 371/4, 8.

voyde *v.* reject, repudiate 240/8; expell, remove 529/20; avoid 298/1; *imp. sg.* free 447/11.

volupe *n.* pleasure 390/8.

vowere *n.* fosterer, patron 244/12.

wayte, wate, wote see **witte**.

wakynge *vbl. n.* keeping vigil 98/4.

walwede *pa.t. 3 sg.* (*refl.*) rolled about 604/15.

-warde *suffix* in *to* (someone, something) -~ towards (someone, something) 43/9, 133/22, 301/10 etc.; *in here-*~towards her 166/10; *into hevene-*~towards heaven 568/15.

ware *adv.* and *conj.* where 291/20, 569/19; **whare** *59/17, 70/12 etc.; when 77/20; wherever 603/11.

wate *adj.* wet 138/2, *410/11.

water(e) *n.*; ~*flode* gushing stream 92/19.

waxe *v.* become, change by growth 431/15; **wex(e)** (no *prep.*) 130/15; *pr. 3 sg. daye* ~*cleere* day dawns 501/8.

wedde *n.* pledge, security 189/22, 192/18, 193/1; *to* ~as a pledge 31/13, 364/15.

weke *n.* week 364/9; **woke** 26/20, 31/7, 336/7, 19.

wele willynge *adj.* benevolent 486/17.

werdelye *adj.* earthly, human 216/16; **wordelye** 218/8.

werye *adj.* habitually on guard 601/9.

werynesse *n.* distaste, tedium 292/13, 600/8, 611/13.

werke *n.* edifice 21/5, 7, 282/3, 15, 20; workmanship 82/18, 96/18.

werkyng(e) *vbl. n.* construction 146/20; workmanship 277/15; **wyrkynge** 172/19; action, operation 72/8; **worschynge** 113/10, 167/2; *be, in* ~ **worchynge** through divine effectiveness 230/3-4, 562/11.

werre *adj.* weary 512/1.

wham *pron.* whom 6/19.

what kynne a *adj.* what kind of 191/3.

whate *adj.* ; ~ *tyme* at the time, when 173/19, 201/11, 233/19; *adv.* how 209/18, 454/14; *pron.* whoever 91/4; whatever 497/15.

whedere *conj.* whether 185/21, 312/8; **whethere** 24/5, 45/24; **wheyþere** 340/18; **where** (contraction) 7/22; ~ *sche may nowʒt* may she not 606/8-9.

whiet, whyet *adj.* white 47/17, 90/16, 120/11, 225/6, 19; lustrous 317/17; **whight** 90/6; **whitter** *comp.* 458/20.

whilke, whylke *pron. rel.* which 345/13, 427/4, 433/10, 440/19; **wiche** 124/10; **whiche a** *adj.* what 12/19, 92/14.

wilfulle, wylfulle *adj.* voluntary 64/1, 266/20.

wilfullye *adv.* patiently, submissively 47/10, 433/14, 482/12; voluntarily 161/7, 580/5.

wille, wylle *n.* determination, intention 39/18, 19, *44/10; desire 63/1; willingness 532/12, 544/13; *atte þi* ~ at your pleasure 222/22; *be here* ~ willingly 601/19-20; *in* ~intending 348/19.

wille, wylle *v.* desire, wish for 56/1, 141/2, 222/19; **whilte** *pr. 2 sg.* 166/2; **wille** *subj. God* ~ *nowʒt* may God forbid 600/8-9; **walde** *pa.t. 3 sg.* 4/18, 5/13,

9/12; **wold(e)** 8/1, 9/8, 12/22; **woldee** 325/2.

willy *adj.* eager, willing 452/10.

wyrke *v.* make, produce 445/16, 548/14; **worche** perform 70/19; act, operate 480/12; **worcheys** *pr. 2 sg.* labor, work 444/4; **werkede** *pa.t. 3 sg.* ached 386/13.

wirschepe, wirscheppe *v.* honour, revere 4/7, 325/2; **worscheppe** 16/16, 25/14.

wysdame *n.* Divine Wisdom 415/12, 422/9.

wyse *n.* way; *in no(o)* ~ in no way, by no means 99/12, 184/22.

wyseeste *adj. sup.* most skillful 197/9.

witte *n.* reason, intelligence 102/9, 151/17; **wittes** *pl.* minds 67/20; senses 48/2, 107/3; **wyttys** mental or spiritual faculties of perception 167/2.

witte *v.* be aware of, know 587/14; **wate** *pr. 1 sg.* 225/12; **wote** 271/19; **wayte** *3 sg.* 24/10; **wate** 312/5; **wyste** *pa.t. 3 sg.* 325/14, 339/16, 605/22.

Wittesonne *n.* Pentecost 215/3.

wittyngelye *adv.* knowingly 601/19.

woke see **weke**.

wondeys *n. pl.* wounds 326/2.

wondere *adv.* very 82/17, 262/2; wondrously 457/19.

wondere *pr. subj. sg.; ne* ~*itt* nor be doubtful of it 611/9.

wondyne *pp.* wrapped up 355/20, 598/4.

woo *n.* misery 310/20.

worldes *n. pl.* ages 155/23; *into alle þe* **worldys, worldeys** for ever and ever 104/15, 393/14.

worschepe *n.* dignity, honour 125/3, 261/15; **wirscheppe** 7/4; *to the* ~ **worschippe** in honour 11/9, 67/7, 10, 478/19; **worscheppe** praise 118/15.

worschepelye *adv.* reverently 388/4.

worschepere *n.* devotee 244/12.

worthynesse *n.* influence 368/23.

wranges *n. pl.* injustices 149/15.

wrastels *pr. 3 sg.* struggles 267/2.

wreth *n.* anger 373/3, 530/2.

wryth *adj.* coiled, twisted *173/10.

Bibliography

Abbot, Thos. K. *Catalogue of the Manuscripts in the Library of Trinity College, Dublin.* Dublin: Hodges, Figgis, 1900.

Allen, Hope Emily. *Writings Ascribed to Richard Rolle, Hermit of Hampole, and Materials for his Biography.* London: Oxford University Press, 1927.

Ancelet-Hustache, Jeanne. *Master Eckhart and the Rhineland Mystics.* Trans. Hilda Graef. New York: Harper Torchbooks, 1957.

——. *Mechtilde de Magdebourg (1207-82). Étude de psychologie religieuse.* Paris, 1926.

The Ancrene Riwle. Trans. M. B. Salu, with an introduction by Dom Gerard Sitwell, O.S.B. London, 1955.

Appleton, LeRoy H. and Stephen Bridges. *Symbolism in Liturgical Art.* New York: Scribner, 1959.

Armstrong, C. A. J. "The Piety of Cicely, Duchess of York: A Study in Late Medieval Culture." In *For Hilaire Belloc,* ed. Douglas Woodruff, pp. 68-91. New York: Sheed and Ward, 1942.

Axters, Stephanus, O.P. *The Spirituality of the Old Low Countries.* Trans. Donald Attwater. London: Blackfriars, 1954.

Bainvel, J. "Cœur sacré de Jésus." *Dictionnaire de théologie catholique.* 3, Part 1, cols. 271-351. Paris, 1938.

Berlière, Dom Ursmer. *La dévotion au Sacré-Cœur dans l'Ordre de s. Benoît.* Paris, 1923.

——. "Le recrutement dans les monastères bénédictins aux XIIIe et XIVe siècles." *Académie royale de Belgique,* 18, fasc. 6 (1924), 5-14.

Birgitta, St. *The Revelations of Saint Birgitta.* Ed. William Patterson Cumming. EETS OS 178. London, 1929.

Blake, N. F. "Revelations of St. Matilda." *Notes and Queries,* 218 (1973), 323-325.

Bloomfield, Morton. *The Seven Deadly Sins.* East Lansing: Michigan State College Press, 1952.

The Book of Vices and Virtues. Ed. W. Nelson Francis. EETS OS 217. London, 1942.

Briquet, C. M. *Les filigranes.* Paris, 1907.

Britt, Matthew, ed. *The Hymns of the Breviary and Missal.* Rev. ed. New York: Benziger, 1924.

Brown, Carleton and Rossell Hope Robbins. *The Index of Middle English Verse.* New York: Columbia University Press, 1943.

Bulloch, James. *Adam of Dryburgh.* London: SPCK, 1958.

Butler, Edward Cuthbert. *Western Mysticism.* 2nd ed. with *Afterthoughts.* London: Constable, 1951.

Cabassut, André, o.s.b. "Une dévotion médiévale peu connue—la dévotion à 'Jésus notre mère'." *Revue d'ascétique et de mystique*, 98-100 (1949), 234-245.

Carthusian Monks of the xiv-xvii Centuries. *Ancient Devotions to the Sacred Heart of Jesus.* Ed. Dom Sebastian Maccabe. 4th ed. London: Burns, Oates, 1953.

Catalogi Veteres Librorum Ecclesiae Cathedralis Dunelm. Surtees Society. London, 1838.

A Catalogue of the Harleian Manuscripts in the British Museum. Vol. 3. London, 1808.

A Catalogue of the Lansdowne Manuscripts in the British Museum. London, 1819.

Catalogue of the Library of Syon Monastery Isleworth. Ed. Mary Bateson. Cambridge, 1898.

A Catalogue of the Manuscripts Preserved in the Library of the University of Cambridge. Vol. 1. Cambridge, 1856.

Chevalier, Cyr U. J. *Repertorium Hymnologicum.* 6 vols. Louvain, 1892-1912; Brussels, 1920-1921.

Chuzeville, Jean. *Les mystiques allemands du xiiie au xixe siècle.* Paris: Éditions Bernard Grasset, 1935.

Clark, Andrew, ed. *Lincoln Diocese Documents, 1450-1544.* EETS OS 149. London, 1914.

Clark, James M. *The Great German Mystics.* Oxford: Blackwell, 1949.

The Cloud of Unknowing and The Book of Privy Counselling. Ed. Phyllis Hodgson. EETS OS 218. London, 1944.

A Collection of Ordinances and Regulations for the Government of the Royal Household. London, 1790.

Colledge, Edmund, o.s.a. "Dominus cuidam devotae suae: a Source for Pseudo-Bonaventure." *Franciscan Studies*, 36/Annual xiv (1976), 105-107.

—— and Cyril Smetana, o.s.a. "Capgrave's *Life of St. Norbert*: Diction, Dialect and Spelling." *Mediaeval Studies*, 34 (1972), 422-434.

Colledge, Eric, ed. *The Mediaeval Mystics of England.* New York, 1961.

—— and Joyce Bazire, edd. *The Chastising of God's Children and The Treatise of Perfection of the Sons of God.* Oxford, 1957.

Coxe, Henry O. *Catalogi Codicum Manuscriptorum Bibliothecae Bodleianae Partis Secundae Fasciculus Primus.* Oxford, 1858.

Deanesly, Margaret. *The Lollard Bible and Other Medieval Biblical Versions.* Cambridge: University Press, 1920.

Deonise Hid Diuinite and Other Treatises on Contemplative Prayer related to "The Cloud of Unknowing." Ed. Phyllis Hodgson. EETS OS 231. London, 1955.

Dolan, Dom Gilbert, o.s.b., "Devotion to the Sacred Heart in Medieval England." *Dublin Review*, 120 (1897), 373-385.

——. *St. Gertrude the Great.* 2nd ed. London, 1925.

Doyle, A. I. "A Text Attributed to Ruusbroec Circulating in England." In *Dr. L. Reypens-Album*, ed. Alb. Ampe, s.j., pp. 153-171. Antwerp, 1964.

——. "The Work of a Late Fifteenth-Century English Scribe, William Ebesham." *Bulletin of The John Rylands Library*, 39 (1956-1957), 298-325.

Dreves, Guido, ed. *Analecta Hymnica Medii Aevi.* Vol. 50. Leipzig, 1907.

Dugdale, Sir William. *Monasticon Anglicanum.* Edd. John Caley, Sir Henry Ellis, and Rev. Bulkeley Bandinel. 6: 1. London, 1846.

Duhr, Joseph. "Communion fréquente." *Dictionnaire de spiritualité ascétique et mystique,* vol. 2, pt. 2 (Paris, 1953), col. 1234-1291.

Durandus. *The Symbolism of Churches and Church Ornaments.* A Translation by John Mason Neale and Benjamin Webb of the first book of the *Rationale divinorum officiorum.* 3rd ed. London, 1906.

The Early English Carols. Ed. Richard Leighton Greene. Oxford: Clarendon Press, 1935.

Eccles, Mark. "*Ludus Conventriae* Lincoln or Norfolk?" *Medium Aevum,* 40 (1971), 135-141.

Eckenstein, Lina, W. *Woman Under Monasticism.* Cambridge: University Press, 1896.

Eden's Fourfold River. Ed. by A Monk of Parkminster. London: Burns, Oates, 1927.

English Mediaeval Lapidaries. Edd. Joan Evans and Mary S. Serjeantson. EETS 190. London, 1933.

Erthe upon Erthe. Ed. Hilda M. R. Murray. EETS OS 141. London, 1911.

Ewer, Mary Anita. *A Survey of Mystical Symbolism.* London, 1933.

Gardner, Edmund G. *Dante and the Mystics.* London: Dent, 1913.

Gertrude, St. *The Exercices of Saint Gertrude.* Ed. by A Benedictine Nun of Regina Laudis. Westminster, Md.: Newman, 1956.

—— and St. Mechtild. *O Beata Trinitas, The Prayers of St. Gertrude and St. Mechtild.* Trans. John Gray. London, 1927.

—— ——. *Revelationes Gertrudianae ac Mechtildianae.* [Ed. Dom Ludwig Paquelin.] Vols. 1 & 2. Paris: H. Oudin, 1875-1877.

Goldschmidt, Ernst Ph. *Medieval Texts and their First Appearance in Print.* London: Oxford University Press, 1943.

Gougaud, Louis. *Dévotions et pratiques ascétiques du moyen âge.* Maredsous, 1925.

Grandgent, Charles. *The Ladies of Dante's Lyrics.* Cambridge, Mass.: Harvard University Press, 1917.

Gray, Douglas. "The Five Wounds of Our Lord." *Notes and Queries,* 208 (1963), 50-51, 82-89, 127-134, 163-168.

——. *Themes and Images in the Medieval English Religious Lyric.* London: Routledge, 1972.

Greene, Richard Leighton, d. *A Selection of English Carols.* Oxford: Clarendon Press, 1962.

Halkin, Francis. "Catalogus codicum hagiographicorum latinorum Paderbornensium et Osnabrugensium." *Analecta Bollandiana,* 55 (1937), 226-243.

Hart, Sr. M. Columba, o.s.b. "Hadewijch of Brabant." *The American Benedictine Review,* 13 (March, 1962), 1-24.

Hendriks, Dom Lawrence. *The London Charterhouse.* London: K. Paul, 1889.

Hilton, Walter. *The Scale of Perfection.* Ed. Dom Gerard Sitwell, o.s.b. London: Burns, Oates, 1953.

Hopper, Vincent Foster. *Medieval Number Symbolism*. New York: Columbia University Press, 1938.

Horstman, Carl, ed. *Yorkshire Writers: Richard Rolle of Hampole, An English Father of the Church, and His Followers*. Vols. 1 & 2. London: Sonnenschein, 1895-1896.

Hymns to the Virgin and Christ, The Parliament of Devils, and other Religious Poems. Ed. F. J. Furnivall. EETS OS 24. London, 1895.

[Jacobus de Voragine.] *The Golden Legend of Jacobus de Voragine*. Trans. Granger Ryan and Helmut Ripperger. New York, 1948.

James, Montague Rhodes. *A Descriptive Catalogue of the Manuscripts in the Library of Peterhouse*. Cambridge: University Press, 1899.

———. *A Descriptive Catalogue of the Manuscripts Other than Oriental in the Library of King's College, Cambridge*. Cambridge: University Press, 1895.

——— and Claude Jenkins. *A Descriptive Catalogue of the Manuscripts in the Library of Lambeth Palace*. Cambridge, 1930-1932.

Jeremy, Sr. Mary, o.p. *Scholars and Mystics*. Chicago, 1962.

———. "Similitudes in the Writing of Saint Gertrude of Helfta." *Mediaeval Studies*, 19 (1957), 48-54.

Jolliffe, P. S. *A Check-List of Middle English Prose Writings of Spiritual Guidance*. Subsidia Mediaevalia, 2. Toronto: Pontifical Institute of Mediaeval Studies, 1974.

Julian, John, ed. *A Dictionary of Hymnology*. 2nd ed. Vol. 1. New York, 1907.

[Juliana, anchoret.] *A Book of Showings to the Anchoress Julian of Norwich*. Edd. Edmund Colledge and James Walsh. Studies and Texts, 35. Toronto: Pontifical Institute of Mediaeval Studies, 1978.

———. *The Revelations of Divine Love*. Trans. James Walsh. New York: Harper, 1961.

Kempe, Margery. *The Book of Margery Kempe*. Edd. Sanford Brown Meech and Hope Emily Allen. EETS OS 212. London, 1940.

Ker, Neil Ripley. *Medieval Libraries of Great Britain*. 2nd ed. London: Royal Historical Society, 1964.

King, Archdale A. *Liturgies of the Religious Orders*. Milwaukee: Bruce, 1955.

———. *Liturgy of the Roman Church*. Milwaukee: Longmans, 1957.

Knowles, David, *The English Mystical Tradition*. New York: Harper, 1961.

———. *The Religious Orders in England*. Vol. 2. Cambridge: University Press, 1955.

Kökeritz, Helge. "Dialectal Traits in Sir Thomas Wyatt's Poetry." In *Franciplegius; Medieval and Linguistic Studies in Honor of Francis Peabody Magoun, Jr.*, ed. Jess B. Bessinger and Robert P. Creed, pp. 294-303. New York: New York University Press, 1965.

Kurath, Hans. *Middle English Dictionary, Plan and Bibliography*. Ann Arbor, 1954.

Leclercq, Jean. "Le genre épistolaire au moyen âge." *Revue du moyen âge latin*, 2 (1946), 63-70.

Ledos, Eugène Gabriel. *Sainte Gertrude*. Paris: V. Lecoffre, 1901.

Lerner, Robert E. *The Heresy of the Free Spirit in the Later Middle Ages*. Berkeley: University of California Press, 1972.

Maddan, Falconer, *A Summary Catalogue of Western Manuscripts in the Bodleian
    Library at Oxford Which Have Not Hitherto Been Catalogued in the Quarto
    Series.* Vol. 4. Oxford, 1897.

Mâle, Emile. *The Gothic Image: Religious Art in France of the Thirteenth Century.*
    Trans. Dora Nussey, from the 3rd French ed. New York: Harper, 1958.

Mann, Horace K. *The Lives of the Popes in the Middle Ages.* 18 vols. London: K.
    Paul, Trench, 1902-1932.

McGratty, Arthur R., s.j. *The Sacred Heart Yesterday and Today.* New York:
    Benziger, 1951.

Mechtild of Magdeburg. *The Revelations of Mechthild of Magdeburg (1210-1297) or
    The Flowing Light of the Godhead.* Trans. Lucy Menzies. London: Longmans,
    1953.

Mechtild, St. *The Love of the Sacred Heart, Illustrated by St. Mechtilde.* London,
    Burns, Oates and Washbourne, 1922.

———. "Mechtildis Virginis Spiritvalis Gratiae." In *Liber Trium Virorum et Trium
    Spiritualium Virginum,* ed. Jacobus Faber, ff. 150^v-190^v. Paris, 1513.

———. *Revelationes Selectae S. Mechthildis.* Bibliotheca Mystica et Ascetica, 10.
    Cologne, 1854.

Meditations on the Life of Christ. Trans. Isa Ragusa and Rosalie B. Green. Princeton:
    Princeton University Press, 1961.

Merton, Thomas. *What are These Wounds?* Milwaukee: Bruce, 1950.

Milosh, Joseph E. *"The Scale of Perfection" and the English Mystical Tradition.*
    Madison, Milwaukee and London: University of Wisconsin Press, 1966.

Moore, Robert. "The Tradition of Angelic Singing in English Drama." JEGP, 22
    (1923), 89-99.

Moore, Samuel; Sanford Brown Meech; and Harold Whitehall. *Middle English Dialect
    Characteristics and Dialect Boundaries.* University of Michigan Publications in
    Language and Literature, 13. Ann Arbor, 1935.

The Myroure of oure Ladye. Ed. John Henry Blunt. EETS ES 19. London, 1873.

Nugent, Sr. M. Rosamund. *Portrait of the Consecrated Woman in Greek Christian
    Literature of the First Four Centuries.* Patristic Studies 64 (1941), diss.
    (Catholic University of America).

"Of the Song of Angels." In *The Cell of Self-Knowledge,* ed. Edmund G. Gardner, pp.
    61-73. London, 1925.

The Orcherd of Syon. Edd. Phyllis Hodgson and Gabriel Liegey. EETS 258. London,
    1966.

Pecock, Reginald. *The Folewer to the Donet.* Ed. Elsie Vaughan Hitchcock. EETS OS
    164. London, 1924.

Poulain, Augustin, s.j. *The Graces of Interior Prayer (Des grâces d'oraison); A Treatise
    on Mystical Theology.* Trans. Leonora L. Yorke Smith from 6th ed. London: K.
    Paul, Trench, 1912.

Pourrat, Pierre. *Christian Spirituality in the Middle Ages.* Trans. S. P. Jacques. Vol. 2.
    London: Burns, Oates, 1924.

Preger, Wilhelm. *Geschichte der deutschen Mystik im Mittelalter*. Vol. 1. Leipzig:
     Dörffling, 1874.

Reynolds, Sr. Anna Maria. "Some Literary Influences in the Revelations of Julian of
     Norwich." *Leeds Studies in English and Kindred Languages*, 7 (1952), 18-28.

Richey, Margaret Fitzgerald, ed. *Medieval German Lyrics*. Edinburgh: Oliver and
     Boyd, 1958.

Richstatter, Karl, s.j., ed. *Medieval Devotions to the Sacred Heart*. London: Burn,
     Oates, 1925.

Robinson, A. Mary. *The End of the Middle Ages*. London, 1889.

Rolle, Richard. *English Writings of Richard Rolle, Hermit of Hampole*, ed. Hope
     Emily Allen. Oxford: Clarendon Press, 1931.

Rowley, Harold H. "The Interpretation of the Song of Songs." In *The Servant of the
     Lord and Other Essays on the Old Testament*, pp. 197-245. 2nd rev. ed. Oxford,
     1965.

S.M.A., o.p. " 'God is our Mother'." *Blackfriars*, 26 (1945), 49-53.

Schroeder, Henry Joseph, o.p. *Canons and Decrees of the Council of Trent*. St. Louis:
     Herder, 1941.

Scott, Edward J. L. *Index to the Sloane Manuscripts in the British Museum*. London,
     1904.

Smalley, Beryl. *The Study of the Bible in the Middle Ages*. Oxford, 1941.

Speculum Devotorum. Ed. Rev. John Banks, s.j. Ph.D. dissertation, Fordham
     University. New York, 1959.

Stierli, Josef, ed. *Heart of the Saviour: A Symposium on Devotion to the Sacred Heart*.
     Trans. Paul Andrews, s.j. New York, 1958.

Suso, Henry. *The Life of the Servant*. Trans. James M. Clark. London, 1952.

——. *Little Book of Eternal Wisdom* and *Little Book of Truth*. Trans. James M.
     Clark. New York, 1953.

Testamenta Eboracensia: A Selection of Wills from the Registry at York. Vols. 2 & 3.
     Surtees Society 30, 45. London, 1855, 1865.

Thompson, E. Margaret. *The Carthusian Order in England*. London, 1930.

Thurston, Herbert, s.j. *Familiar Prayers: Their Origin and History*. Westminster, Md.:
     Newman, 1953.

Tyson, Moses. "Hand-List of Additions to the Collection of Latin Manuscripts in the
     John Rylands Library, 1908-1928." *Bulletin of The John Rylands Library* 12
     (1928), 581-604.

Underhill, Evelyn. *Mysticism*. New York: Noonday, 1955.

——. "Medieval Mysticism." In *Cambridge Medieval History*, 7: 777-812.
     Cambridge, 1932.

Vernet, Félix. *La spiritualité médiévale*. Paris, 1929.

Walsh, James. "God's Homely Loving." *The Month*, N.S. 19 (1958), 164-172.

Watkin, Aelred. "Some Manuscripts in the Downside Abbey Library." *The Downside
     Review*, 59 (1941), 75-92.

Webber, Fred Roth. *Church Symbolism*. 2nd ed. Cleveland: Jansen, 1938.

Wenzel, Siegfried. *The Sin of Sloth: "Acedia" in Medieval Thought and Literature.* Chapel Hill, 1960.

Williams, Margaret Anne. *Glee-Wood: Passages from Middle English Literature from the Eleventh Century to the Fifteenth.* New York: Sheed and Ward, 1949.

Wills from Doctors' Commons. Edd. J. G. Nichols and J. Bruce. Camden Society 83. London, 1863.

Woolf, Rosemary. *The English Religious Lyric in the Middle Ages.* Oxford, 1968.

Woolley, Reginald Maxwell. *Catalogue of the Manuscripts of Lincoln Cathedral Chapter Library.* London, 1927.

Wormald, Francis. "The Revelation of the Hundred Pater Nosters." *Laudate,* 14 (1936), 165-182.

Young, Karl. *The Drama of the Medieval Church.* 2 vols. Oxford: Clarendon Press, 1933.

Index to *The Booke of Gostlye Grace*

(Numbers in parentheses identify the line(s) on
the page cited for which there is a Note.)

Index to the Introduction

OTHER BOOKS ON THE MEDIEVAL CHURCH...

Edmund COLLEDGE and James WALSH, eds. *A Book of Showings to the An-choress Julian of Norwich.* (Studies and Texts 35.) 1978; viii, vi, 789 pp.

J. J. Francis FIRTH, ed. *Robert of Flamborough, Canon-Penitentiary of Saint-Victor at Paris. Liber poenitentialis.* A critical edition with in-troduction and notes. (Studies and Texts 18.) 1971; xxx, 364 pp.

P. S. JOLLIFFE. *A Check-List of Middle English Prose Writings of Spiritual Guidance.* (Subsidia Mediaevalia 2.) 1974; 253 pp.

Phyllis Barzillay ROBERTS. *Stephanus de Lingua-Tonante. Studies in the Sermons of Stephen Langton.* (Studies and Texts 16.) 1968; xii, 271 pp.

Michaeal WINTERBOTTOM, ed. *Three Lives of English Saints.* (Toronto Medieval Latin Texts 1.) 1972; x, 94 pp.

PONTIFICAL INSTITUTE OF MEDIAEVAL STUDIES
59 Queen's Park Crescent East
Toronto, Canada M5S 2C4

Write for our latest catalogue